Science for Craft Potters and Enamellers

Science for Craft Potters and Enamellers

Kenneth Shaw

DAVID & CHARLES : NEWTON ABBOT

ISBN O 7153 5525 2

For Isabel

Set in 11 point Baskerville
and printed in Great Britain
by W. J. Holman Limited   Dawlish
for David & Charles (Publishers) Limited
South Devon House   Newton Abbot   Devon

CONTENTS

LIST OF ILLUSTRATIONS

Plates

In the Text

PREFACE

This is a book for the hobbyist, craftsman and artist wishing to understand something of the simple science of ceramics. It is written for those who wish to delve beneath the surface of the practical procedures involved in the shaping, finishing and firing of clay and metals that make up potting and metal enamelling.

The beginner (for whom a glossary is included) as well as the skilled craftsman should find in this book much that is essential to the successful working of these materials, for there is no doubt that the production of fine ceramic art is possible only when the artist understands the processes, especially in firing, that give ceramics their unique characteristics.

Most potters and enamellers learn by trial and error. This book offers a quicker way to the knowledge of the processes of ceramics. It provides the reader with clear explanations of what happens when clays, metals and glasses are prepared, shaped and heated. The possession of such information should enhance the probability of success and satisfaction, whether the aim is to enjoy a hobby, produce gift articles for friends, or to develop ceramic skills as the basis of earning a living.

Numerous accounts already exist on the art of throwing, design in ceramics and simple shaping methods, and so in this book such topics have been largely ignored except where they need to be touched upon in order to describe the theory and the science. Discussions with craftsmen and careful reading of their own accounts and questions have pointed the way to the subjects that cause the most trouble in the workshop. This treatment of these aspects will, I hope, solve some of the common problems of potting and enamelling. But more than this, the book may form the foundations on which a thorough understanding of ceramic science can be built.

Craft ceramics is a growing activity in schools, colleges, evening classes and in the home. The marketing of simple kits, especially for making attractive jewellery and other arte-facts, has aroused widespread interest in pottery and metal enamelling. The transition from 'tinkering' at home to loftier ambitions and the creation of artistic designs in clay and metal calls for more detailed information and knowledge. It is hoped that this book will provide that knowledge in a concise, easily read form.

Schools, whose art and craft curricula include pottery or enamelling—or both—may find the book helpful in stimulat-ing their pupils to learn the principles of ceramic science and in doing so to make better pots and enamels.

KENNETH SHAW
Brixham, September, 1971

section 1

MATERIALS

1 CLAYS AND METALS

The more he likes to think of himself as an artist, the closer the ceramist works with truly raw materials, those substances that he digs, quarries or produces in other ways from where nature laid them. Between the artist, for whom chemical processing means denaturing his materials, and the factory worker, for whom it means increasing efficiency and avoiding faulty products, there are many types of craftsman.

In this book the sections describing raw materials and their properties are written for clay and enamel workers who wish to understand the nature of the substances of ceramics, since to the artist, as to the industrialist, a knowledge of the physics and chemistry cannot but benefit the product.

Whatever their needs as to quality, both the industrialist and the craftsman use a great number of raw materials. Clays, feldspar, chalk, metallic ores and oxides and many more are processed, blended and fired in a variety of ways to make up the ceramist's palette of materials.

Clay is to the potter what metal is to the enameller. Indeed, the making of pottery and enamelled ware have much in common. Both consist of a body and a skin: the clay and the glaze; the metal and enamel. Each combination must be selected so that its parts can coexist during the shaping, firing and decorating processes. Too much incompatability causes the glaze to flake off the body or crack; the enamel behaves likewise toward the metal.

The raw materials used in making glazes—the glassy skins applied to pottery, and in making enamels—are the same. All such glassy skins are based on a framework of silica. Glazes and enamels share the use of such substances as sodium, potassium, boron, calcium, iron, aluminium, titanium and lead, to name only the common elements of ceramic practice and science. Figure 1 shows the structure of glazed pottery and enamelled metal.

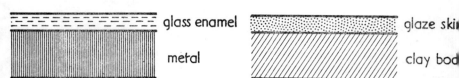

glass enamel   glaze ski
metal   clay bod

Fig 1 Glazed ceramics and enamelled metal, showing the similarity in structure between the two. Each consists of an underbody and a glass skin. The intermediate layer is more highly developed in the pottery and glaze structure than in the metal-enamel structure

The above list contains the names of chemical elements but the potter is unlikely to see boron or calcium in their elemental states; what he does see and touch are the clays, minerals, glasses and metals of the earth and of man's ingenious processing and regeneration—the products of the metallurgical and chemical industries.

In handling these materials, the ceramist is eager to discover their properties: how they can be shaped, dried and fired; how they can be cut, carved, scratched and painted on. In examining glaze making materials or frit-producing substances, he wishes to know how long it takes the furnace to fuse them into glasses, if pigments will be stable in them and if the resulting vitreous skins can be persuaded to adhere to the clay or metal without cracking.

Tests have been devised to predict the likely behaviour of these materials. Later, some of these tests will be described so that the newcomer to the subject can experiment and open up new fields of creativity and effect.

PLASTIC MATERIALS

Clays and Kaolins

The commonest types of plastic clay used in ceramics are those based on kaolinite. Kaolinite is the mineral of a very white, slightly plastic clay which does not readily fuse in a potter's kiln, ie, kaolin or china clay. Kaolinite is a complex mineral, usually represented simply by the formula Al_2O_3.

$2SiO_2.2H_2O$. Most china clays, fireclays, ball clays, stoneware clays, fusible clays, red clays, vitrifiable clays, boulder clays, loams, marls (malms) gaults, shales and others are based on, or contain proportions of, the mineral kaolinite.

Origin of clay

Clays of interest to the ceramist come from three types of rock: 1. *Igneous,* yielding granite which in turn yielded kaolins *see under* 3. 2. *Sedimentary,* deposited as a sediment by rivers and glaciers. The materials in the sediment originated from the weathering of older rocks. Ball and similar plastic clays such as fireclays and stoneware clays were so formed. 3. *Metamorphic,* altered by heat and pressure in the earth's crust to yield, for example, china clays from granite. The process is known as pneumatolysis.

Properties of clays

Why are clays plastic, and what is plasticity? A plastic clay is one that can be blended with a certain critical amount of water and worked (pressed and kneaded) into a condition enabling it to be shaped or moulded so as to retain that shape during drying.

Plasticity depends on the shape and size of the particles that make up the clay and the presence of fine carbon matter (blue and black ball clays contain varying amounts of carbonaceous matter). Certain minerals can be obtained as extremely fine particles and these are called 'colloidal'. In this ultrafine state, very small quantities in a clay will have a very marked effect on the plasticity and slip-casting properties of clays (see under: *Casting Slips*).

This account of plasticity also explains why some clays, formed in different ways, are more plastic than others. Kaolins (china clays) found in Georgia, South Carolina and Florida (USA); Cornwall (England); Czechoslovakia; and Prosyanovsk (USSR) are much less plastic than ball clays and certain fireclays. Kaolins are called *primary* clays because they are found at their sources of origin. Another description for them is *residual* because they reside where they were formed from the parent rock.

Clays that are much more plastic than kaolins usually owe

their plasticity to having geen geologically transported from
the place of origin and deposited elsewhere (a second resting
place). Hence they are called *secondary* or *sedimentary* clays.
During this movement the clays are ground very finely and
are contaminated from contact with other minerals. However,
secondary clays during their segregation by water and ice and
their subsequent sedimentation and purification, lose the bulk
of the impure residue of the parent rock. They thus contain
a lower percentage of impurities but often have a greater
variety of impurity. Since many of these impurities in secondary clays are colorants, such as iron, manganese and titanium,
the clays when fired are cream, brown or even red, compared
with the whiteness of a good quality primary clay (kaolin).

Table 1 shows the chemical analysis of some common primary (china) and secondary (ball and fire) clays from which we
note the contaminating effect of the geological transportation
process described above.

Table 1. *Chemical Composition of Some Clays (%)*

Oxide	Kaolin (China Clay)	Ball Clay	Fireclay (Stourbridge)	Red-Burning	Cambridge Marl
SiO_2	47.0	48.8	65.0	63.0	17.0
TiO_2	—	1.4	0.3	0.6	0.2
Al_2O_3	38.5	33.6	22.0	20.0	7.0
Fe_2O_3	0.8	2.5	2.0	6.0	0.3
MgO	—	0.6	0.5	—	—
CaO	—	1.2	0.3	—	41.5
K_2O	1.1	1.7	0.1	2.7	0.4
Na_2O	0.6	0.8	0.2	2.7	0.5
Loss on ignition	12.0	9.4	9.0	5.0	34.0
SO_3	—	—	0.6	—	—

Interpreting clay composition

Chemical analyses such as those shown in Table 1 are obtained in the laboratory. The tests involve calcining (firing)
the sample of clay which has been dried at 110°C and weighing it to determine its 'loss on ignition'. That is, the content of
organic materials and water that will burn out of a clay when
it is fired. This is followed by chemical analysis to determine
the inorganic (that is, noncombustible) substances. Looking at
the list of oxides given in Table 1, SiO_2 (silica), Al_2O_3 (alum-

ina), CaO (calcium oxide), and so on, the potter might think that clays are simply mixtures of oxides, and that clays could be synthesised simply by blending these metallic oxides in the required ratio. This is not true. Clays are not mixtures of oxides and they cannot be synthesised by mechanical mixing.

Clays are mixtures of complex aluminosilicates occurring only in nature and usually characterised by plasticity when blended with water. Most clays contain some free silica (as quartz) and other impurities that have important effects on ceramic properties. It is the very different types and amounts of impurities and the varying proportions of the main aluminosilicates (compounds of aluminium, silicon and oxygen), together with the different particle shapes and sizes, that give the potter his very wide range of clays. From this it follows that two clays having the same chemical analysis (expressed as oxides) may have quite dissimilar properties in terms of plasticity and fired colour—to mention only two important properties.

A classical example will help to clarify this point. *Halloysite* is a clay mineral belonging to the same group as kaolin, that is, the kaolinite group. Like kaolin it has the same number of alumina and silica units, but halloysite has four water molecules compared with kaolin's two:

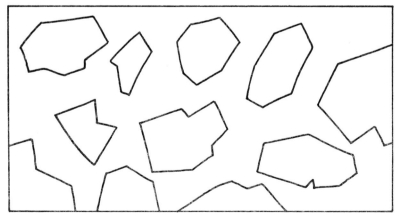

Fig 2 Sketch of outlines of kaolin particles as seen under the electron microscope, showing the flat, plate-like structure of the grains of clay, a property that explains distinctive properties such as plasticity

B

Kaolin $Al_2O_3.2SiO_2.2H_2O$
Halloysite $Al_2O_3.2SiO_2.4H_2O$

However, the particles of kaolin (china clay) are flat and plate-like (see Fig 2). When they are moved about during plastic working, the water added for potting acts as a lubricant, enabling the kaolin platelets to slide over each other, making the material more plastic. On the other hand, the crystal particles in halloysite are not flat but tubular (see Fig 3) owing to the rolling of the sheet structure (too small to be

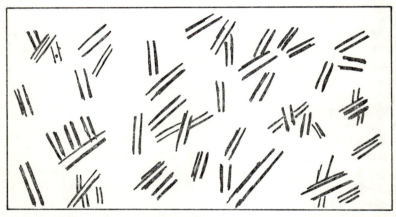

Fig 3 Sketch of particle shapes in halloysite mineral present in some clays, as seen under the electron microscope. Contrast the particle shape with that of kaolin in Fig 1. When the tiny tubular particles of halloysite collapse in firing, excessive high shrinkage of the clay-ware occurs

seen by the naked eye). Not only are halloysite clays less plastic than kaolins but also, during drying and firing, the behaviour is also quite different. Instead of showing a gradual and moderate shrinkage in drying and firing, halloysite shows an irregular and sudden shrinkage as the water is driven off and the microscopic tubes collapse.

Halloysite clays are found in New Zealand, Japan, North Africa and Missouri (USA).

Binding power

The capacity of a plastic clay to absorb a nonplastic material such as quartz sand, feldspar, or grog (burnt clay, known also as chamotte) is often related to its plasticity, though the two properties are not comparable. The binding power of the clay is important to the craft potter who may wish to throw large articles on the wheel and needs to give strength and support to the otherwise floppy plastic clay. Adding grog is like giving the flesh a skeleton.

Mechanical (green) strength

The term 'green' is used to describe clayware that has been shaped but not yet fired. The green or mechanical strength of clays is important not only in enabling shaped ware to preserve its form during drying and transporting, but also to facilitate further processing, such as turning on the lathe, carving and scraping by hand and glazing and painting. Green strength is closely related to plasticity. Highly plastic clays are usually stronger in the green dried state than low-plasticity clays.

Shrinkage

When plastic clay is allowed to dry, it loses the water that has been added to it to make it plastic. As the films of water between the platelets of the clay leave the drying article, these platelets move together and pack themselves more tightly. Shrinkage is important for several reasons:

1 Shrinkage must be controlled if cracking is to be avoided.
2 Ceramic articles that must have a given size must be designed taking into account the amount of shrinkage.
3 Shrinkage sometimes takes place to different extents in different directions (that is, it is nonisotropic), depending on the way the article was shaped: extruded from a pugmill, cast, thrown, and so on.

Plastic clays usually shrink more than low-plasticity clays and so the potter may add grogs or other inert fillers to his clays to reduce the shrinkage. Grog-clay combinations dry more evenly and quickly because the system is opened up to the passage of moisture.

Fired shrinkage

When dried clays are fired they usually shrink. Some clays expand, but these are much rarer and their use is normally

confined to the making of special, expanding firebricks for
furnace linings. Shrinkage must be taken into account in designing specifically sized articles and the firing cycle designed
so that the hot shrinkage is not too sudden or excessive, otherwise squatting and deformation may take place.

Simple tests on clays

Testing the green and fired shrinkage of clays consists in
mixing a sample of dry clay with a known amount of water,
shaping a block, say $12 \times 6 \times 3$cm, marking a given length in
the plastic, newly moulded state; drying and measuring; and
finally firing the piece, followed by the third and final
measurement.

Chemical composition

If the physical properties of clays—their particle sizes and
shapes—affect the plasticity and workability in moulding as
well as other 'green' properties, then it is equally true that the
chemical properties will affect their behaviour during firing.
Accordingly, the way in which a clay behaves during firing
will affect the functional properties of the ware.

In other words, the chemical behaviour, which also includes
the types of minerals present, their proportions, and the way in
which they react together during heat processing, determines
the final properties of the ceramic: its hardness, strength, resistance to cracking, surface finish and other properties. For
example, firing a pot at too low a temperature so that the body
does not vitrify (glassify) means it will be porous and mechanically weak. For any kind of pot, there must be some degree of
glass formation (or sintering, which is incipient vitrification,
the development of glass on the periphery of the particles
undergoing heat treatment) in order to convert the clay ware
into a ceramic article.

For a given firing cycle, that is, the temperature and time
for which the pottery is subjected to that temperature, it will
be the chemical composition of the body that will have the
most critical effect. Each of the oxide constituents mentioned
in Table 1 has a particular effect or performs a certain task in
a clay body. The mineral which contributes the particular
chemical oxide is also important. Thus, in other words, clays

having different mineral compositions but the same chemical oxide compositions may behave in different ways.

The potter, let us suppose, has discovered what appears to be a promising clay near his workshop and wishes to develop a body suitable for his particular product and firing conditions. On the other hand, perhaps he wishes to modify his conditions to suit the new clay.

First it will be necessary to blend the clay with water and sieve it—a 40s screen should be satisfactory—to remove roots and large stony matter. Having allowed the sieved slip to stand in a tub, after a few days some of the water may be siphoned off. The rest can be dried off either with gentle heat or by pouring the slip on a plaster of Paris slab (Fig 4) and allowing

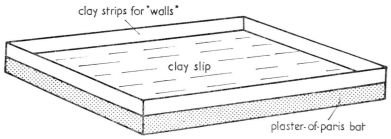

Fig 4 Clay slip can be dried out after purification by sieving and magneting if it is poured on to slabs of plaster of Paris as shown here. The plaster bat absorbs the water turning the slip into plastic clay. Bats must be dried out after use

the plaster to suck up the water. The resulting soft clay can then be used to shape test pieces (see above) for drying and firing shrinkage tests.

These samples can also be used to give information on green and fired strength, green and fired colour, presence of iron pockets, and presence of lime nodules.

A typical record of the above procedure is shown in Table 2.

TABLE 2

Date	Name of clay	Dry Shrink-age %	Fired Shrink-age %	Green Appear-ance	Fired Colour	Firing Temp (°C)	Remarks

This information can be supplemented by other data such as binding capacity, which is measured by rolling a weighed portion of clay in sand or fine grog to determine how much sand can be absorbed before the clay loses its plasticity. If the clay is to be used for casting slips, the amounts of chemical deflocculent (see under *Casting Slips*) needed to produce satisfactory fluidity can be determined and recorded. Table 3 shows the layout of such a record.

TABLE 3

Date	Name of clay	Pint Weight	Composition of Slip Clay Spar Others	Chemicals Soda Sodium Ash Silicate	Remarks

The casting-up time for a given body thickness and other slip properties can also be measured. It is also useful to measure the fluidity and thixotropy of casting slips on a simple instrument such as a torsion viscometer. The next stage is to make some pots and fire them. Modifications may be necessary both to improve the working properties (additional grog to open up the clay) and to alter the behaviour of the clay in the kiln (additions of quartz to confer crazing resistance).

Effect of impurities

Alkalis, such as soda, potash and lithia, act as fluxes to reduce the melting point of the clays. Too high a content of alkalis may cause distortion and twisting of the product in firing. Mica, which contributes alkalis, is often stained with iron and may cause specking and other types of discolouration.

Most natural clays contain quartz in varying amounts. The general effect is to increase the fusion point of the clay but quartz has certain other important effects which will be discussed below. Sandy clays contain large quantities of quartz which often make them difficult to work in the plastic state.

Organic matter is not detrimental as it usually burns out on firing and may confer certain advantages such as enhanced plasticity or stable casting slips.

Soluble salts such as potassium sulphate and various alums tend to cause trouble in casting. They may produce scumming and other faults on the clay ware. High soluble-salt concentrations sometimes lead to trouble in glazing, causing the glazes or even underglaze colours to refuse to adhere to the ware.

The effect of weathering on clays, a practice which is not often carried out to-day, was to break up the clay, improve the plasticity, increase the raw clay porosity and wash away soluble salts. It also oxidised the iron pyrites and facilitated its manual removal, and converted the iron sulphide into sulphate, making it soluble and removable by washing.

Types of clays

Ball clays and kaolins are the commonest commercial clays used in the pottery industry. Other clays found locally may be used by craft potters and artists for their ware. A wide range is available from suppliers who provide chemical analyses, firing temperatures, colour, shrinkage and other information. High-grade kaolins fire very white, contain about 5% free quartz, and 1·5-2% fluxes, mainly as mica.

The alkali fluxes such as soda and potassia (Na_2O and K_2O) are the remains of the granites from which kaolin is derived. If a very refractory kaolin is required, the alkali concentration should be as low as possible in order to prevent the formation of fusible compounds. Organic matter in kaolins such as coal or lignin is not disadvantageous providing it burns out so as to give a white clay. Highly organic clays are often more plastic and make better casting slips than those free of carbonaceous matter.

In blending industrial bodies (a commercial earthenware body, for example, contains four ingredients: ball clay, china clay, Cornish stone or feldspar, and flint) the content of free quartz that is, silica SiO_2 in the china clay, must be known and taken into account.

A rough idea of the free quartz content is obtained by sieving a weighed amount of raw clay through a 60s screen under running water after the clay has been thoroughly blended with water. The quartz can be distinguished from the mica and other ingredients of the residue by comparing them with known samples. The estimation of free quartz, that is, silica that has not been combined chemically with the clay and fluxes during firing, is important, since it is the free quartz that determines the crazing resistance and strength of ceramics (see Section IV).

Ball clays

These cannot be used without the addition of other ingredients because of their very high shrinkage and cracking propensities. The unfired colour cannot be used to judge the fired colour as black ball clays owe their colour to organic matter which burns out in firing and which makes the clay plastic, also stabilising the casting properties. The purest types of ball clays (the name 'ball clay' comes from the old practice of cutting the clay into balls for transporting) are considered to be the blue clays of South Devon in England. Mixtures of various types of ball clays have for many years formed the basis of the pottery industry of Stoke-on-Trent, England, and of other ceramic centres. Other world pottery clay areas include Kentucky and Tennessee in the USA.

The metal enameller uses ball clays to keep nonplastics, such as frits, in suspension for spraying onto the metal, and for glass and pigment making.

As in china clays, the effect of alkalis in ball clays is to reduce the fusing point and make the fired clays more glassy. Iron oxide will colour the clays from cream, through ivory and brown, to a distinct red, depending on the other ingredients of the clay. Titanium dioxide, TiO_2, is especially important in conjunction with iron oxide since iron is a much stronger pigment in its presence.

The effect of the other clay ingredients on the colouring power of iron is illustrated in Table 4.

TABLE 4

COLOURS FROM IRON OXIDE IN DIFFERENT
CLAY ENVIRONMENTS*

Oxides in Clay	Fired Clay Colour
1-5% Fe_2O_3 1-8% CaO Low Al_2O_3	Oxidising fire gives red; reducing fire gives buff, pink or grey
1-10% Fe_2O_3 10-25% Al_2O_3 0-1% CaO	Reds of all shades; harder firing introduces a purple tint

1-3% Fe_2O_3 25-30% Al_2O_3 No CaO	Buff or straw colours

*The presence of TiO_2 invariably intensifies the pigmentary power of the Fe_2O_3.

Effect of lime on clays

The effect depends on the quantities present. Marls contain very large amounts of lime. Small amounts act as a flux by combining with silica to give calcium silicate.

Albany clays

These are plastic clays found near Albany, New York, USA. They are readily fusible because of their high alkali (K_2O, Na_2O) content and are commonly used in the USA as engobe and glazing materials. They also contain moderate amounts of calcium and magnesium oxides. Fired onto stoneware as slips they yield brown glazes. Albany clays are members of the fusible group of clays found throughout the world and commonly used by craftsman potters. Small quantities can sometimes be used as vitrifying agents in low-temperature bodies and even in stoneware bodies.

Brick clays

These are widely used for making building ceramics. Those selected for commercial production need to be plastic for mechanised moulding. They usually vitrify at 900-1100°C but should not produce excessive glass concentrations that might cause squatting. Brick clays are usually highly contaminated with iron, calcium and other impurities that render them quite unsuitable for potting, although certain purer beds may be used for rough earthenware, especially if covered with engobes or opaque glazes.

High-lime brick clays in which the lime is intimately mixed with the clays vitrify very quickly at around 1000°C, and begin to shrink even at 860°C. The colour of brick clays depends on the composition and especially the iron and titanium contents (see Table 4).

Boulder clays

Also known as glacial clays, these have variable compositions depending on the journey made by the glaciers from which they were deposited, but are without the refining effect of sedimentation. During the journey, the boulder clay may have picked up lime which is often present in lumps. Like all secondary clays they are fine grained and plastic. They show marked drying and firing contraction and fuse at low temperatures due to their high flux contents (calcia, potash and soda, iron and titania). If used for potting, boulder clays need to be purified mechanically to remove grit, gravel and other rock materials.

Red clays

Where the glacier has passed over iron-bearing surfaces the boulder clays may be excessively contaminated with iron oxide in various forms. The resulting clay may then be a red clay which when processed is suitable for making red pottery such as Rockingham Ware (teapots) and Terra Cotta.

The iron compounds in clays suitable for potting must be either finely dispersed in the clay or chemically combined with the aluminosilicates (in the form of solid solutions) if the colour of the fired ware is to be uniform and pleasing. Fremington clays found in North Devon are probably iron-stained boulder clays.

Triassic marls (Keuper marls) are also often red burning. Containing only small amounts of lime, which tends to bleach the colour of some marls, these clays are suitable for making Terra Cotta and similar red bodies. Some triassic clays are also suitable for making blue engineering bricks (a reducing firing is required for these products).

Calcareous clays

These are high in lime which may be present in various forms, eg finely dispersed, and therefore acting as a vigorous flux and bleaching the iron colour, so that a strong red fired body may be difficult to obtain, especially if high fired. Commercial, low-temperature bodies are prepared by adding large amounts of lime to conventional earthenware mixtures. Such bodies are common in the tile industry. Majolica bodies, which are porous and usually covered with opaque tin glazes, also have high contents of lime. Similar pottery bodies are Delft Ware and Faience. The lime-clay bodies in this general classification are normally fired at temperatures below 1000°C.

Lime occurring naturally in the clay may be present as lumps or nodules and is then difficult to deal with. If the lime is not dispersed by grinding, the fault of lime blowing may arise during firing of the ware. This is manifest in the flaking-off of small pieces of the article (in the biscuit or even in the glazed state).

Upon coming into contact with moisture, either from the atmosphere or from the glaze in dipping, lime is hydrated, giving:

$$CaO + H_2O = Ca(OH)_2 + heat \ (15,900 \ cal)$$

The lime may also be present as calcium sulphate (gypsum). Similar effects may be noted, although much higher temperatures are needed to decompose the gypsum, $CaSO_4$, compared with those needed to break down the calcium carbonate, $CaCO_3$.

Where possible, it is advisable to avoid using high-lime natural clays for making craft pottery for the above reasons and also because the lime content is likely to vary considerably from batch to batch. The firing range of calcium clays is short, and squatting may result if temperatures are not carefully controlled.

Fireclays

This class of clay, like building clay, is wide ranging and used, as the name implies, to make heat-resistant bricks and shapes for furnaces and kiln construction, for saggars and kiln furniture, for sanitary ware and acid-resistant building materials, and also in buff-coloured tiles.

Iron-free fireclays, which are quite rare, may be suitable for certain types of high-fired pottery though most fireclays are coarse. The plasticity may be high, though siliceous fireclays are not easily moulded by pottery making methods. It was for a long time considered that fireclays are mostly based on the kaolinite mineral form, with a large number of impurities, including high concentrations of carbonaceous matter and iron oxide. However, it is now known that in many fireclays the principal mineral is either intermediate between kaolinite and halloysite; or there is a mixture of the two (sometimes also including other minerals).

Fireclays also exist in the flinty or the nonplastic state which, when mixed with water, have very little plasticity. These are quite unsuitable for pottery making except possibly as grogs and fillers. The term 'fireclay' is usually reserved for materials fusing at temperatures of at least 1580°C.

Like kaolins, fireclays were formed chiefly from gneisses and granites. Weathering first caused these rocks to break down into feldspar, quartz and mica. Then under the action of aqueous solutions of carbon dioxide (carbonic acid), deeper and more effective decomposition occurred in the mica and feldspar. The feldspar breakup can be represented as follows:

$$K_2O.Al_2O_3.6SiO_2 + 2H_2O + CO_2 =$$
$$\text{feldspar} \qquad Al_2O_3.2SiO_2.2H_2O + K_2CO_3 + 4SiO_2$$
$$\text{kaolinite}$$

The potassium carbonate, K_2CO_3, so formed is soluble in water and is removed in due course by leaching, while the kaolinite and quartz (SiO_2) remain to form kaolin (china clay).

As stated, halloysite with the formula $Al_2O_3.2SiO_2.4H_2O$, may form instead of kaolinite (see under *China Clay*, above).

Other minerals found in fireclays include monothermite, $O.2R_2O.Al_2O_3.3SiO_2.1·5H_2O$ (note: R_2O stands for K_2O and Na_2O); some clays also contain montmorillonite, $Al_2O_3.4SiO_2.nH_2O$ (that is, a variable number of molecules of water in its crystal).

The monothermite mineral results from the weathering of hydrated micas in the parent rock. Montmorillonite is present in bentonites, which are highly plastic, soapy clays used in small amounts in glazes and slips to aid suspension.

Pyrophyllite may also result from the above reactions $(Al_2O_3.4SiO_2.H_2O)$, and is present in many clays.

It may be instructive to compare fireclays with secondary kaolins used in fine potting (ball clays). It is found that the iron oxide content in the secondary kaolins may be very low (less than 0·2%), while in fireclays it reaches 3-5%. The alkali content (K_2O, Na_2O, MgO and CaO) is also low in kaolins, often hardly totalling 1·5%, whereas in fireclays it is frequently as much as 4%.

China clays (kaolins) usually retain traces of the parent rock from which the kaolinite was formed (quartz, feldspar and mica). However, such impurities, except quartz are often absent from fireclays. While kaolin can be processed to remove these impurities to yield 95-98% pure kaolinite (also called clay substance), it is normally impossible or economically impracticable to so purify fireclays.

The temperatures at which fireclays fuse to give a hard dense mass are roughly proportional to their alumina (Al_2O_3) contents and, industrially, fireclays are classified by this factor. The higher the Al_2O_3 content of a material or fired refractory, usually the higher its refractoriness. Fireclays are also widely used for making grogs, though for the potter they are often too badly stained with iron. Calcined ball clays may be more suitable. The effects of the various chemical compounds are similar to those in other less refractory clays. Silica, however, reduces the fusing point of aluminous fireclays, whereas highly siliceous potter's clays may be quite refractory. Alkalis, iron, magnesia and calcia all reduce the refractoriness of fireclays.

Loams are high in sand or gravel. They are usually poor potting clays. *Marls* are heavily lime contaminated clays frequently burning red. See above under calcareous clays. *Shales* are compressed, flinty clays that do not readily develop plasticity. They are of little interest to the potter except possibly as grog. Some highly refractory shales are included in the fireclay class of materials.

Stoneware clays

These are vitrifying clays similar to some ball clays but having such a wide range of colour, composition and properties that it is difficult to generalise about them. Indeed, most potters at some time work in a plastic stoneware body for throwing or other fabrication method, simply because this type of clay is very responsive to the aims of the potter's art.

Many craftsmen say that better all-round results come from blending a variety of stoneware clays rather than adding non-plastics such as flint or feldspar to a single clay.

A typical clay composition range for stoneware, vitrifying at 1120-1180°C is: 50-67% SiO_2, 21-32% Al_2O_3, 0.5-2.5% TiO_2, 0.8-8% Fe_2O_3, 0.1-2.5% CaO, 0.02-1.5% MgO, 0.2-3% K_2O,

0.1-2.5% Na_2O, and 6-12.5% loss on ignition.

Stoneware clays should be free of gypsum and iron pyrites, which would cause lime blowing and iron spotting on the surfaces of the ware, and also of high soluble-salt concentrations which might cause surface flashing (that is, vitrification at the surface of the ware while the underbody remains porous).

Red clays are discussed under brick clays and stoneware clays.

2 METALS FOR ENAMELLING

The art enameller uses a wide range of hard and soft metals for producing decorative and functional articles. The range of metals includes steel, cast iron, aluminium, copper, silver and gold, and special alloys. Bronze and brass cannot be effectively enamelled.

Because of the recent growth in art enamelling, the use of the medium for architectural and other large murals and panels, involving the use of large areas of metal, suppliers have been willing to develop alloys and steel grades specifically for enamelling. Metal suppliers will also sometimes cut batches of blanks and shapes for small users. Fig 5 shows some shapes commonly used by enamellers.

Enamelling techniques

Successful technique in enamelling depends, as in all arts, on knowing the potential and limitations of the materials available, and working within those limitations. As a practical example, enamelling on aluminium has great potential, not only because the metal is an excellent constructional material, light in weight and resistant to weather, but also because recent metallurgical developments have made its use more extensive and economical.

Architects interested in the finish of their buildings are showing mounting interest in aluminium, finished in a variety of ways, for features on the façades of public buildings, churches, and the interiors of halls, railway stations and stadia.

Cast iron

Grey cast iron is commonly used for enamelling, although white cast iron was once thought to be the only suitable iron for this process. Grey cast iron is an alloy of iron and carbon with a total carbon content of 3·25-3·60%. The best cast irons for enamelling have an ideal carbon content of about 3·30%. Impurities remaining in grey cast iron from the blast furnace in which the iron ore was smelted include manganese, silicon, phosphorus and sulphur.

Table 5 shows typical chemical compositions of irons used for enamelling.

TABLE 5
SOME CHEMICAL COMPOSITIONS OF
ENAMELLING IRONS (%)

Elements	Domestic and Decorative Ware	Baths, etc	Chemical Apparatus
C	3·5-3·7	3·4-3·6	3·3 -3·5
Si	2·4-2·8	2·2-2·6	2·0 -2·4
Mn	0·5-0·6	0·5-0·6	0·5 -0·6
P	0·4-0·5	0·3-0·4	0·12-0·25
S	0·15	0·12	0·0

Effect of impurities

Silicon makes the molten iron more fluid and also softens the casting by causing graphite to be precipitated. Phosphorus also increases the fluidity and helps in shaping thin castings, say for plaques and murals. Manganese tends to weaken the harmful effects of sulphur which reduces the cast strength and makes the casts shrink too much.

Design of castings

Sharp corners and edges on which the fired enamel would chip must be avoided. Uniform heating in the enamelling furnace is also needed, and the metal distribution in the casting must be taken into account.

Many simple shapes such as flat wall plaques, ash trays and 'contemporary' shapes, of course, can be cast and enamelled without special difficulty. Large numbers of such articles are made as standard lines for the art enameller and individuality is conferred on them by the surface finish, in the choice of enamel colours, pattern and unusual techniques.

Cast iron made for enamelling should be dense and have a

clean surface, free from mould sand, slag inclusions, gas and shrinkage cavities. Once a particular enamel has been found suitable with a given cast iron, changes in the enamel composition should be made with great care, since different iron structures may require different enamel compositions and firing treatment.

The thermal expansions of coating and metal must match, if flaking and other faults are to be avoided. Thermal expansion depends on the structure as well as the composition. For instance, the structure of white cast iron is quite different from that of grey iron, and one enamel composition is unlikely to suit both equally well.

Sheet steel

In describing ferrous sheet materials for enamelling, metallurgists often use the term 'sheet irons and steels'. Cast irons and steels are all alloys of iron and carbon, the final properties depending on the amount of carbon, its form, and the methods used to process the alloys, as well as the impurities.

In addition to being cut, sheet steel can be welded, thus extending the range of forms for the artist. Welding must be done before the metal surface is treated prior to applying the enamels.

The compositions of enamel-stock sheet steel are very similar to those of mild steels. They should be not more than 0.02% in silicon. Other impurities are manganese, chromium, nickel, phosphorus, sulphur and oxygen.

Sheet steel that is to be cold stamped and welded should be highly ductile and have a high thermal conductivity, factors which depend on composition, for the purer the steel the greater the ductility and thermal conductivity. A good low carbon enamelling steel would have the composition: 0.05-0.12% C, 0.25-0.5 Mn, less than 0.04% P, less than 0.04% S, less than 0.33 Ni, and less than 0.15% Cr.

Titanium steels

Steels containing 0.5-0.7% titanium are now being used for enamelling without the need to apply ground enamels. The advantages claimed for titanium steel are: better sag resistance in the enamel kiln and a better finish. It is customary to

C

give titanium steels a nickel dip in the pickling process if the ground coat is omitted.

The structure of enamelling steel should be fine grained, free of non-metallic inclusions and between 0·35 and 0·60 mm for artware. The surface should be smooth and crack free. Since the bonding or adhesive strength between the ground coat and the enamel and the metal is controlled by the degree of oxidation (rusting) of the steel when the articles are being fired, the extent to which the steel surface can be oxidised is important. If the oxidising effect is too weak, it causes ultimate flaking of the enamel, while steels that strongly oxidise are prone to faults such as burn-off and copper heading (red-brown spots).

Aluminium

The development of satisfactory glass enamels suitable for coating aluminium has opened up a wide front for the use of this valuable constructional material. It can also be used for murals, plaques, containers, assemblies, mosaics and other decorative forms.

Aluminium sheet can be shaped by cutting and shearing, drilling, filing and other metalworking methods. The metal's surface is particularly suitable for receiving a vitreous enamel. Aluminium is light in weight (specific gravity 2·7), and fairly cheap. The thermal-shock resistance of enamelled aluminium is high. A very wide range of thicknesses is available, from foil to castings.

Recent developments in leadless enamels for application to aluminum, and the expansion in aluminium rolling have made aluminium a very exciting medium for the art and craft enameller, especially for large scale work, eg interior murals and dividing walls for public buildings, in the home, aboard ships, even in aircraft and trains.

Properties of aluminium

High mechanical strength, electrical and thermal conductivity make aluminium very suitable for enamelling. It resists corrosion much better than iron and mild steel because, when exposed to the atmosphere it forms on itself a protective film of aluminium oxide (Al_2O_3). However, should this film be dissolved or attacked by corrosive, especially acid or alkaline, substances, the metal becomes pitted and tarnished. By enamelling it is possible to protect the surface of aluminium against the effects of most corrosive substances.

One outstanding feature of enamelled aluminium is its cracking resistance even when bent beyond its elastic limits. The bond between the enamel layer and the metal, providing the glass is not too thick, is very strong. The enamelled aluminium shapes can be drilled, cut, bored and bent within certain commonsense limits.

The thermal-shock resistance of the enamel coats applied to aluminium is greater than that of those applied to steel. Specimens of glass coated aluminium have been rapidly cooled from 500-600°C to 20°C without flaking or cracking. Because of this it is also possible to weld the reverse sides of enamelled aluminium articles, for instance, in order to secure plaques and other items to constructions and walls.

Aluminium alloys

These are suitable for enamelling and can be bought as castings and as wire, rods, pipes and sheet. All forms should have the maximum possible melting point in order to facilitate firing of the applied enamel, and they should also have smooth surfaces, a property which is readily achieved with such an obliging metal.

The composition of aluminium alloys is carefully controlled in production, and the essential requirement of low impurity content is usually met. A standard enamelling aluminium produced for industrial purposes and suitable for craft enamelling would contain 98-99% Al and less than 1·6% Mn. The total remaining impurities, mainly silicon, iron and copper, would amount to not more than 0·7%.

The most successful results are obtained with *sheet aluminium* which is easily shaped. Castings frequently contain gas and non-metallic inclusions which cause faults in the enamel coating during firing, such as pinholing, when the gas escapes. The easiest shapes to enamel are tiles, panels and trays.

Corrugated or crimped aluminium

This is often used for enamelling to prevent deformation

during firing and cooling. Sheet gauges range from 0·3 to 3·0 mm. It is also possible to apply vitreous enamels to *aluminium foil*, though special knowledge is needed to retain the coherence of the enamel foil structure. In industry the foil is enamelled by a continuous method of rolling and spraying, followed by firing. The foil is 0·2-2·0mm thick and the enamel coating 0·07mm thick. The enamelled foil is used for technical (for instance, electrical engineering) purposes but has distinct decorative possibilities for the painstaking craft enameller, and can be rolled on to drums.

Copper

The newcomer to art enamelling and especially if the craft is to be practised on a very small scale, say at home or in school, will probably start with copper enamelling. It is an easily worked metal, relatively cheap, takes enamels very well, and as it melts at a high temperature (1084°C) it can be fired in the enamelling furnace quite successfully without the need for great skill. The range of surface effects with copper, both in the natural state and after applying clear glasses, is very great.

Copper is a soft ductile metal that does not easily corrode in the atmosphere. It can be extended by hammering and other metalworking techniques. Suppliers sell a wide range of sheet, bars, tubing and wire. Some suppliers will provide mixed collections of stamped shapes ready for enamelling or for further final shaping before enamelling by the craft worker. Figure 5 shows some common shapes obtainable from most metal suppliers.

It is usual to purchase cold rolled annealed copper that has a fine finish, free of pitting and heavy scratches. Roofing copper which is a zinc-copper alloy, is unsuitable for enamelling since it cracks and blisters in the kiln.

Some suppliers in the USA will provide sheets of copper that carry attractive surface effects made during rolling and other processing, in the form of stars, hatching and line patterns. In Europe, a copper made for enamelling contains 5% zinc and gives excellent results and can be enamelled without a ground coat.

Since art enamelling on copper usually calls for several fir-

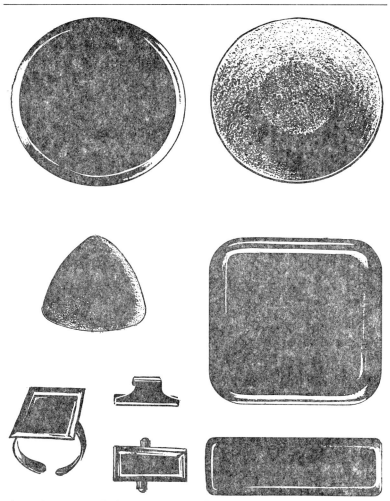

Fig 5 Some metal shapes and 'findings' (jewellery fittings) supplied for vitreous enamelling by the British suppliers, Wengers Limited of Stoke-on-Trent. Similar shapes are available from American and other suppliers

ings for different colours, the copper sheet should be quite thick in order to ensure that the article will maintain its shape during repeated firings. A sheet about 1/16in thick is recommended for good quality multicoloured copper enamelled work. To save expense and especially for trials, school work, and for once-fired articles, thinner sheet can be used. Usually the heavier the gauge of sheet the better the tactile qualities of the finished piece.

Gold and its alloys

Gold melts at 1064°C and, when suitably alloyed for expensive jewellery, it is an excellent enamelling metal base. Pure gold is rather soft, and jewellery items can be easily bent or otherwise distorted. It is customary to alloy it down to at least 92% gold and 8% other metals (22 carat). Other gold alloys are: 1. 88% Au, 12% Cu. 2. 66·7% Au, 8·3% Cu, 25% Ag. 3. 66·7% Au, 3·3% Cu, 30% Ag.

Gold is fully recoverable even if the enamelling turns out to be unsuccessful. The colours and glasses can be removed with acids such as hydrofluoric, which will not affect the gold. The only agent that will dissolve gold is *aqua regia*, which is a mixture of nitric and hydrochloric acids.

Silver

The surface of silver, which melts at 961°C, should not be completely covered by enamels (why use silver when steel will suffice if the entire surface is to be enamelled?), but should be enhanced by using clear enamels, sometimes tinted with delicate blues (cobalt) and green (chromium stains). A typical jewellery silver alloy contains 92·5% silver and 7·5% copper. This alloy has a lower fusing point than pure copper, and special care is needed in firing, if softening, blistering and other faults are to be avoided.

Other metals

Bronzes and brasses are not easily enamelled and should be avoided since they offer the artist no real advantage over those metals discussed above. Platinum is used in the jewellery trade but is usually too costly for enamelling. A silver-platinum alloy containing 5% platinum has been used for some costume jewellery, but the process is difficult owing to the high thermal expansion of platinum. This leads to stresses being set up in the enamel-metal structure and there is a great tendency for the glass to flake off the base metal. Guilder's metal is a copper-zinc alloy (9-10% zinc). The effects with it are excellent when skill is applied, but faults are frequent because of the zinc which seems to be incompatible with the enamelling process and blisters the ware.

3 FLUXES AND GLASS-FORMING MATERIALS

Pottery bodies and many other ceramic materials, including enamels, contain some glassy or vitreous constituent. For a long time it was thought that earthenware, for instance, was made up of particles of silica, surrounded by films of glass that had been formed during the fusing and vitrifying of the clay and fluxes of the mix. It was customary to attribute a distinct role to each of the ingredients of a ceramic body, so that it was thought silica made the skeleton, clay gave plasticity and body, and the flux (feldspar, Cornish stone and such materials as whiting or nepheline syenite) contributed the glassy cement that bonded all the other ingredients into a hard strong *ceramic* mass.

We now know that the firing of pottery produces a much more complicated pattern of events than this. The roles of the ingredients are not so simple and it is impossible to think of each raw material as acting independently.

Glasses in pottery

It is useful for the potter to consider the precise laws formulated by the glass technologist in order to explain the behaviour of glass-forming raw materials. The advantage for the potter is that in many cases those raw materials are common to both industries. To quote one example, H. Moore, the eminent glass technologist, considered that pottery glaze making consisted in modifying a window glass composition to give it a suitable softening and flowing temperature without impairing its durability too much. A list of potter's fluxes used in ceramics with their molecular formulae (see Appendix 1) is given in Table 6.

TABLE 6

Name of Flux	Molecular Formula	Use
Soda-feldspar (albite)	$Na_2O.Al_2O_3.6SiO_2$	Bodies, glazes, enamels
Lime-feldspar (anorthite)	$CaO.Al_2O_3.6SiO_2$	Bodies, glazes, enamels
Apatite	$Ca_3(Cl.F.OH)(PO_4)_3$	Glazes and enamels
Barium carbonate	$BaCO_3$	Glazes and enamels
Borax	$Na_2B_4O_7.10H_2O$	Glazes and enamels
Borocalcite	$CaO.2B_2O_3.6H_2O$	Glazes and enamels
Boric Acid	H_3BO_3	Glazes and enamels
Calcite	$CaCO_3$	Glazes, bodies, enamels
Cryolite	Na_3AlF_6	Glazes and enamels
Dolomite	$CaCO_3.MgCO_3$	Glazes and enamels
Fluorspar	CaF_2	Glazes and enamels
Galena	PbS	Glazes (toxic)
Lepidolite	$(Li.K.Na)_2.(F.OH)_2$	Glazes and enamels
Lithium Carbonate	$LiCO_3$	Glazes and enamels
Magnesite	$MgCO_3$	Glazes and enamels
Nepheline syenite	$K_2O.3Na_2O.4Al_2O_3.$ $8SiO_2$ and feldspar	Bodies, glazes and enamels
White Lead	$Pb(OH)_2.2PbCO_3$	Glazes and enamel frits
Witherite	$BaCO_3$	Glazes and enamels
Whiting	$CaCO_3$	Bodies, Glazes and enamels
Sodium Carbonate	$Na_2CO_3.10H_2O$	Glazes and enamels
Soda Ash	Na_2CO_3	Glazes and enamels
Red Lead	Pb_3O_4	Glazes and enamel frits
Potassium carbonate	K_2CO_3	Glazes and enamel frits
Lead Bisilicate frit	$PbO.2SiO_2$*	Glazes and enamels

*Commercial frit contains some Al_2O_3

Fusing of solids

The manner in which a solid such as feldspar or lead bisilicate fuses when heated is important to the ceramist. A distinction must be made between the sudden precise melting of a pure compound such as frozen water and many potter's materials, for the latter are not pure, but mixtures of several compounds. Indeed it is a good thing for the ceramist that his raw materials do not fuse suddenly and at a precise temperature. It is an advantage that they gradually soften over a long range of temperature. Imagine the effects if a pot were solid at say 999°C and molten at 1001°C. The potter would have no control over his firing, and failure to begin cooling at 1000°C would mean pools of liquid would form on the bottom of the kiln. The enameller would find his materials so fluid that it would be impossible to make them stay on the metal long enough to fire them.

Vitrification range

Of course some ceramic raw materials do melt or fuse much more quickly than others. Potash feldspar, for example, is considered to fuse over a shorter temperature range than sodium feldspar or calcium feldspar. In other words, once the materials begin to soften in the heat it takes some of them longer to become fluid than it does others providing the speed of raising the temperature remains constant.

The terms 'sharp' flux and 'sluggish' flux are often used to describe this behaviour. Adding potassium oxide to a glaze will produce different effects depending on the compound used. We can use either potassium carbonate, K_2CO_3, which is a sharp flux with a distinct melting point, or potash feldspar which, although a sharper flux than calcium feldspar, is a sluggish flux compared with potassium carbonate.

Ceramic blends are heated in order to bring about the desired chemical and physical changes which transform clay into pottery, or change raw materials into glaze or enamel frit. It is the heat that causes these changes and, eventually, a rising temperature would melt or burn any raw material or mixture of materials known to man.

The aim of the ceramist is to apply enough heat—and no more—so as to cause the desired changes to take place; to stop or arrest the reactions in the melting mass at the critical stage. That stage is reached when the new ceramic possesses all the desired properties. In the past the reactions taking place in the firing of clay ceramics were known as 'arrested reactions'.

Overfiring and underfiring

Taking away the heat from a clay body before all the desired changes have occurred means the material is underfired or immature. This means the fluxes have not done their work and the cold, fired ceramic may be porous, chalky and weak. In an enamel or glaze, underfiring may mean the coating is not shiny, or that it has bubbles of gases still on the surface. Even lumps of undissolved, unfused sand and feldspar may protrude above the surface.

Overfiring, applying heat for too long, or allowing the temperature to rise too high, may cause the essential reactions in the blend to continue beyond the desired point. The fluxes become excessively fluid and start to attack the other ingredients too fiercely so that, instead of merely bonding them into a hard strong ceramic mass, they dissolve them excessively and turn the entire mass into glass. The result is deformation or slumping of the ware, or blistering of the glaze or enamel. Sometimes the ware bloats or even explodes.

Composition and heat

The ceramic process consists therefore in matching the chemical compositions of the raw mixtures to the amount and fierceness of the heat applied in firing. By controlling these two factors the ceramist is able to take from his kiln a product with the desired combination of properties: hardness, durability, strength, impermeability to liquids, smooth finish, stable colour, and attractive or beautiful appearance.

4   GLASS-FORMING REACTIONS

Glasses may be transparent or opaque, solid, hard, and brittle with a range of valuable properties. The potter thinks of his glazes as thin films of glass applied to a clay body to protect and beautify it. The enameller uses a wide range of frits and glasses that can be pulverised and applied to metals, followed by fusion in a furnace. When cold and solidified they cover, protect and beautify the metal bases.

To define glasses in a precise way is much more difficult. One way out of the problem is to call them *supercooled liquids* because they do in fact resemble liquids in many ways. But probing into the structure of glasses, attempting to discover how the atoms and molecules are put together, leads us to contradicting evidence. The above definition becomes rather over-simplified and in many ways unsatisfactory.

Fritting process

Certain glazes and most enamels are fritted. Raw materials such as sand, soda ash, potash and clay are melted together in a pot furnace or fritting kiln (Fig 6). This makes glasses out of raw materials some of which are soluble in water. If these soluble materials such as soda ash, potash, lithium carbonate, borax or boric acid, were mixed with water and the insoluble raw materials, such as clay, feldspar and sand or flint, added in order to make a glaze or enamel, the mixing water would dissolve some of the soluble materials, making it impossible to obtain a homogeneous glaze or enamel.

In lead-glaze manufacture it is also important that all raw lead compounds such as red lead be turned into glasses to prevent the danger of lead poisoning in humans, since red lead and certain other lead compounds will dissolve in the acids of

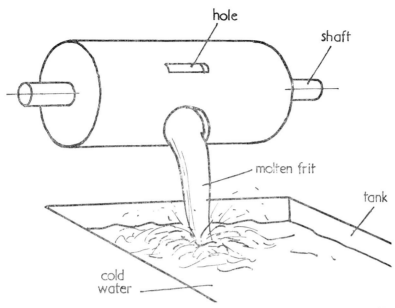

Fig 6 Frit-Making. The molten glass or frit is melted in a rotary kiln lined with refractory bricks, and is then poured into cold water to granulate it ready for milling

the human stomach and cause toxicity. The answer to this problem is to render the lead insoluble by melting it with glass-forming raw materials.

Silicate science

The whole technology of ceramics was once covered by the term 'silicate technology'. In recent years the word 'ceramic' has now become generally used to involve many important strategic and engineering materials that do not contain any silica at all. Alumina, borides and carbides are examples.

Ceramics, glasses and enamels are mixtures of silicates. It is true that we may start with other compounds such as oxides or carbonates or sometimes fluorides. But we inevitably finish up with combinations and mixtures of silicates. A simple glass-forming model may serve in any attempt to understand the firing of ceramics and the melting of frits and glazes.

Quartz (flint or sand, SiO_2)

The other ingredients of the blend will combine with the silica to form complex silicates. During these reactions, or before they start, the silica undergoes certain changes in itself. These are called crystal inversions, in which the arrangement of the atoms of silicon (Si) and oxygen (O) in the crystal of silica is modified, causing changes in the amount of space occupied by the structure. Sometimes the space is less, after shrinkage, at other times it is greater, due to expansion.

At room temperature, sand or flint (quartz) is called 'alpha-quartz'. Upon heating this changes into other forms of quartz. The processes are usually represented thus:

$$573°C \qquad\qquad 870°C \qquad\qquad 1470°C$$
$$\alpha - quartz \rightleftarrows \beta - quartz \rightleftarrows \alpha - tridymite \rightleftarrows cristobalite$$

The temperatures over the arrows indicate the temperatures at which the changes occur, and these particular types of arrows indicate that the changes take place reversibly, that is both when the temperature is being raised and when it is being lowered. One of the forms of silica in the change series, tridymite, can exist in its own family of forms, called alpha-bet- and gamma-tridymite. The precise form assumed by tridymite depends on the temperature environment in which it finds itself. The changes are usually represented thus:

$$117°C \qquad\qquad 163°C$$
$$\gamma - tridymite \rightleftarrows \beta - tridymite \rightleftarrows \alpha - tridymite$$

As they are about to change, the silica forms are less stable and more ready to form stable structures with the accompanying ingredients of the melt. Understanding the way in which silica changes its form in heating is the key to many practical problems in pottery, ceramics and enamelling.

The series of changes is not even now complete, for cristobalite, the third main form of silica, also wishes to have more than one identity. Its behaviour is represented by:

$$198-274°C$$
$$\alpha - cristobalite \rightleftarrows \beta - cristobalite$$

Cristobalite finally gives up the desire to change is guise, and at $1713°C$ fuses into glass.

Sodium carbonate (Na_2CO_3, soda ash)

Soda ash is the calcined form of sodium carbonate, familiar

to the housewife as washing soda. Upon heating, washing soda loses its water of crystallization thus:

$$Na_2CO_3.10H_2O \rightarrow Na_2CO_3 + 10H_2O\uparrow$$
$$Na_2CO_3 \rightarrow Na_2O + CO_2$$

In the furnace melting our imaginary glass or frit, the soda ash melts at 852°C. But long before that, at 400°, it loses about 0·33% of its weight through volatilization. Volatilization is the process of removing by heat, in the gaseous form, some of the components of the glass or ceramic batch. It explains why the starting constituents of ceramic batches are not always precisely the same as the final composition of the product. Many materials are removed in the furnace by volatilization, mainly alkalis, lead, and such compounds as sulphides, selenium compounds in pigments and others.

Potassium carbonate (K_2CO_3, potash)

This melts at 897°C. The reaction during heating is as follows:

$$K_2CO_3 \rightarrow K_2O + CO_2$$

Sodium sulphate (Na_2SO_4)

This, like silica, changes its crystal form. At 239°C it changes from the rhombic to the monoclinic form, which are different forms of the sodium sulphate crystal. At a much higher temperature, around 1200-1220°C it dissociates (decomposes) thus:

$$Na_2SO_4 \rightleftarrows Na_2O + SO_3$$

This process continues up to 1350°C before it is complete. The soda (Na_2O) will rapidly combine with some of the silica (SiO_2) to form sodium silicate, a vigorous flux that soon starts to dissolve other materials such as kaolin and more silica to produce the complex silicates mentioned above.

Ceramists are well aware of the often novel effects of *reducing* atmospheres on their products, a condition achieved on purpose or accidentally by starving the process of oxygen. One of the effects of reduction at this stage of the glass-forming reaction would be to cause the above breakdown of sodium sulphate to take place at a much lower temperature (about 530-590°). The strong soda flux would therefore become available at a much lower temperature.

Whiting (chalk, limestone, calcite. $CaCO_3$)

The fineness of raw materials, that is, the size of the particles, affects the firing processes. Simply, the finer the materials the faster the reactions. This is because reactions occur at the surfaces of the particles and the finer one grinds a powder the more one increases its surface area.

This principle is clearly illustrated with calcium carbonate (whiting) added to a frit batch. The effect of heat is to decompose the carbonate thus:

$$CaCO_3 \rightarrow CaO + CO_2$$

This makes available the flux CaO to react with other ingredients such as silica to form calcium silicates. However, the rate of this breakdown in whiting depends on the particle size of the raw whiting. Ground to a particle size of 0·06mm the whiting loses 36% of its carbon dioxide, while a particle size of 0.09mm reduces the loss to 22% (both samples were heated at 610°C for 60 hours). The researchers who obtained these data thus state that temperature is more important than time in this important fluxing reaction.

Magnesium carbonate, $MgCO_3$

This may also be added as dolomite. It is easily decomposed into magnesia and carbon dioxide according to the reaction:

$$MgCO_3 \rightarrow MgO + CO_2$$

The breakdown occurs most vigorously at 620°C, and produces the flux MgO for reaction with silica and other materials in the same way as CaO.

Dolomite, $CaCO_3$. $MgCO_3$

This breaks down at 700°C and provides CaO and MgO as highly reactant fluxes in the mass being heat processed.

Barium carbonate, $BaCO_3$

This behaves in a way similar to calcium carbonate in that it ultimately provides a reactive flux, BaO, for subsequent glass-forming processes. However, upon heating it behaves in a more complicated fashion than whiting. It first forms a basic salt, $BaO.BaCO_3$, which subsequently breaks down into barium oxide (baria, BaO) and carbon dioxide:

$$2BaCO_3 \rightarrow BaO.BaCO_3 + CO_2 \qquad (1)$$
$$BaO.BaCO_3 \rightarrow 2BaO + CO_2 \qquad (2)$$

Barium does not find common use in ceramic fluxes or enamel frits and it is confined to high-temperature glazes such as some porcelain types where it is necessary to make the glaze of more complex compositions in order to facilitate fusing. For instance, barium oxide might be added to a raw glaze with whiting and feldspar to make a sluggish high-temperature glaze with which to coat fireclay bodies. Barium carbonate is toxic.

Sodium nitrate (saltpetre, $NaNO_3$)

This fuses at 318°C and then at 350° onwards dissociates to give off oxygen:

$$2NaNO_3 = 2NaNO_2 + O_2$$

Potassium nitrate, KNO_3

This melts at 336°C and then at 500°C breaks up into the nitrite and oxygen. Above 500°C, the nitrite decomposes into potassium oxide, K_2O, nitrogen and oxygen (compare the reactions given for sodium nitrate).

Boric acid, H_3BO_3

This is a common flux in glazes and enamels, though it is more expensive as a source of boron than borax. The advantage for glass and frit making is that boric acid does not bring with it the sodium oxide accompanying the use of borax. Some frits in which the sodium oxide constituent is contributed by feldspar would be too high in soda if borax were used. When heated to 100°C, boric acid gives up some water and at higher temperatures forms boric oxide, B_2O_3, the form in which it is reported in frit and glaze formulae, (see also under glazes and enamel frits).

Borax ($Na_2B_4O_7$. 10 H_2O)

This, also called sodium diborate or tetraborate, contributes sodium as well as boron to the glass or glaze. It is used in the granular form in enamelling, and as powder and grains in glass and glaze making. Borax contains 36·52% B_2O_3, 16·25% Na_2O and 47·23% water (of crystallization). When heated

D

borax progressively loses its water of crystallization. At about 61°C it loses five of the molecules of H_2O, and at 320°C it has changed from the hydrated form completely into anhydrous (without water) borax, $Na_2B_4O_7$, which fuses at 714°C. The importance of using hydrated borax in fritting is well known. The water of crystallization, upon heating, leaves the borax and, vigorously boiling through the mass, helps to homogenise it, and accelerates the process. In addition, hydrated borax starts to fuse at 100°C, and the resulting fluxing effect can begin so much earlier. In comparison the dehydrated form does not fuse until 740°C.

Red lead (Pb_3O_4)

This is a very valuable flux in frits. It should not be used in the raw (unfritted) state, as it is toxic and can cause lead poisoning in humans if it enters the blood stream through the acids of the stomach. When heated, red lead decomposes to form lead oxide PbO and oxygen thus:

$$2Pb_3O_4 \longrightarrow 6PbO + O_2$$

Kaolin ($Al_2O_3 . SiO_2 . 2H_2O$)

Like silica (SiO_2), kaolin is one of the essential components of glasses and frits since it cheaply contributes alumina in addition to silica. The fluxes described above combine with it to yield the fundamental silicates (or aluminosilicates) which make up ceramic materials. The effect of heat upon kaolin is considered in detail in Section IV. Briefly, at about 600°C the water of crystallization ($2H_2O$) has been driven off and the rearrangement of the mineral's molecules commences.

Feldspars

These contribute potassium and sodium oxides, alumina, and silica. Albite (soda feldspar) fuses at 1100°C, orthoclase (potash spar) at 1170°C, and anorthite (calcium feldspar) at 1550°C. The essential reactions commence with fusion and the formation of corrosive liquids which attack the other ingredients of the batch (body, glass or glaze), followed by decomposition and combination with other oxides present.

The firing or fusing of a ceramic or enamel blend involves a series of complex physical and chemical reactions that take place simultaneously or one after another, at different velocities, and with the products of each set of reactions having an effect on the subsequent reactions. The whole process is *dynamic*, on the move, and changing all the time. This property, coupled with the fact that the reactions are occurring under heat, gives us the idea of *thermodynamic reactions*—an excellent description of what takes place in the heat treatment of glass and enamel materials (and all forms of ceramics).

Before describing the rest of the raw materials used as fluxes and glaze-forming agents it may therefore be instructive to list the reactions and their temperatures when a typical glass batch, containing four materials, is heated over a temperature range of 240-1200°C. This will provide some idea of the kinds of reactions that occur in many forms of ceramics and enamels.

Fusion composition

Let us consider the silica-soda-calcium-magnesium system. Raw materials in the forms of carbonates and quartz can be used to produce the following oxide composition:

72·6% SiO_2, 15·2% Na_2O, 8·7% CaO and 3·5% MgO.

During heating and subsequent study the following reactions occur in the mixture:

1 Formation of double salts of magnesium and sodium carbonate at below 300°C.
2 $MgCO_3$ starts to break down at 300°C.
3 Formation of double salts of calcium and sodium carbonates starts at below 400°C.
4 $CaCO_3$ starts to break down at 420°C.
5 Magnesium and calcium silicates form with sodium silicate (fluxes) at 340-700°C.
6 Carbon dioxide gas evolves at 340-900°C.
7 Vigorous reaction between soda ash and silica to form sodium silicate at 700-900°C.
8 Whiting reacts with silica to give calcium silicate and CO_2 at 600-920°C.
9 A liquid appears due to the formation of a eutectic* between magnesium and soda silicates and silica and the double carbonates at 780-880°C.
10 Magnesium oxide combines vigorously with silica to form

magnesium silicate at 980-1150°C.

11   Similar reactions for calcium oxide to yield calcium silicate at 1010-1150°C.

12   $CaSiO_3 + MgSiO_3 \rightarrow CaSiO_3.MgSiO_3$, 600-1200°C.

13   The melt dissolves the grains of quartz, calcium silicate and magnesium silicate at 1150-1200°C.

*When mixtures of materials are heated it is found that a certain combination of constituents fuses at a lower temperature than any other combination for that system. This mixture is called a *eutectic*, and it exhibits the minimum melting point.

Even with only four oxides in the mixture the ceramic or glass-forming process involves many complex reactions before the transformation from raw to fired (vitrified) material is complete. When another oxide (or perhaps a sulphide or fluoride) is added to the mass, the degree of complexity is enhanced. In the firing of ceramics and enamels it is common to use as many as eight or nine oxides, introduced by such means as clays, carbonates, oxides, pigments, mineral fluxes and ores. Although it is often convenient to ascribe a certain simple property to a material, to say, for example, that soda reduces the fusing point of enamels; or calcium makes clay bodies vitrify more quickly, it is important to note that such statements may not be valid for all conditions. The picture is much more complicated. For the working ceramist the aim must be to understand and apply the theory of silicate science to his own conditions and materials.

5   OTHER NONPLASTICS:
POTTERY BODIES

The potter may now ask about clay bodies, in which the essential reactions cannot be allowed to go so far as to lead to full vitrification and liquid glass development. In porous earthenware bodies, for instance, with porosity values of from 12% to 25% or more, the appearance of the fired body suggests that there has been little or no vitrification in the sense that fluxes have melted and dissolved the grains of quartz and clay.

It is true that full vitrification has not occurred in such bodies. However, many of the reactions described above for glass melting do occur, or start to occur, when bodies are fired. And the higher the firing temperature and the longer the soaking times in the kiln, the greater the extent of such reactions.

Wollastonite

This is a calcium metasilicate, $CaSiO_3$, which melts at 1544° C. The form found in natural deposits (beta-form) is used in wall-tile bodies and low-temperature earthenware bodies for art ware and similar ceramics. If natural wollastonite is fired at about 1100°C, a new form, known as the alpha-form, is produced. It is also known as pseudo-wollastonite.

High-strength bodies can be made by fluxing wollastonite with barium carbonate and adding about 20% plastic clay. Such compositions fired at 1200-1250° to give a highly vitrified body are used in the electrical ceramics industry. The mineral sometimes forms as needle-like growths in ordinary calcareous bodies, contributing to the mechanical strength of the material.

Fluorspar

This has the formula CaF_2 and melts at 1360°C. This is not a suitable material for body fluxing, although experiments have been done on its mineralising action in industrial ceramics, that is, its power to accelerate mineral formation in the firing of such bodies. It is used as a vigorous flux in enamels and glasses and also in developing certain ceramic and enamel frits and colours but a practical hazard is that fluorine gas, volatilized from the material, attacks the structure of the kiln or furnace, causing rapid wear. Fluorspar is present in varying small amounts in unprocessed Cornish stone. Manx stone, similar in properties to Cornish stone and found in the Isle of Man, is relatively free of fluorine. Cornish stone is also now treated to remove much of the impurity, including fluorine and iron.

Talc, $3MgO. 4SiO_2. H_2O$

This is a mineral that in the massive natural form is called steatite. Technical steatite ceramics find extensive use in electrical engineering. Talc is used as a flux in tile and similar earthenware bodies; these are known as cordierite bodies.

The oxide composition of talc is as follows (%): SiO_2 58-60.5, Al_2O_3 2-4.5, $Fe_2O_3 + FeO$ 3-5.5, MgO 28.5-30 and K_2O 0.27-0.8.

Talc is useful in making volume-stable thermal-shock resistant bodies, and reducing various faults such as dunting, and even glaze faults such as crazing. Talc therefore finds use in making flame-proof and oven-to-table ware. Partly the effect is due to talc's ability to convert the quartz to cristobalite; the latter increases the crazing resistance of glazed ceramics. In the USA talc is widely used in glazed wall tiles.

However, it must be used carefully since certain talc-clay mixtures have very narrow vitrification ranges, leading readily to distortion in firing. Better control over materials, processing and especially firing than are used with feldspar bodies is essential.

The reactions occurring in ceramic bodies when talc is added are complex and illustrate the principles outlined above in the section on silicate formation. The amount of liquid formed in talc-clay bodies can vary rapidly with temperature owing to the complexities of the phases in the $MgO - Al_2O_3 - SiO_2$ diagram.

Talc is also used as a glaze flux to incorporate magnesia and may sometimes reduce crazing in glazes. The effect on the fluidity of the glaze is important. Talc makes glazes viscous and, like other magnesium materials, is useful for preventing running and 'curtaining' faults, and to prevent underglaze colours flowing into the glaze.

Nepheline

This is a fluxing mineral similar to feldspar but containing less silica. The material is mined as the rock nepheline syenite which contains nepheline, feldspars, but no free silica. Nepheline is used in the USA to make vitrified bodies because of its sharper fluxing properties compared with either feldspar or Cornish stone. For bodies already having a high proportion of free silica, nepheline may be a useful flux to replace some of the feldspar or stone.

The formula for nepheline is $K_2O.3Na_2O.4Al_2O_3.9SiO_2$. But the rock nepheline syenite, the material that is crushed and sold to ceramists and enamellers, contains microcline, albite and mica.

Dolomite

This is a double carbonate of magnesium and calcium with the formula $CaMg(CO_3)_2$. The material used by the ceramist and glass maker is a rock composed chiefly of this mineral in which the ratios of $MgCO_3$ and $CaCO_3$ may vary considerably. Dolomitic limestone is the term used to describe rocks having a high proportion of limestone.

Pure mineral dolomite contains 45·7% $MgCO_3$ and 54·3% $CaCO_3$, yielding 30·4% CaO, 21·9% MgO, and 47·7% CO_2 in terms of oxides. Natural dolomites often contain iron and other impurities making them coloured, from buff to red and even black or blue. Other impurities are silica (quartz), feldspar, mica and clay.

When heated to 600-650°C dolomite is decomposed into basic oxides. The reaction is spread over a temperature range of 250-300°C and takes place in two stages:

$$CaCO_3MgCO_3 = CaO_3 + MgO + CO_2 \qquad (1)$$
$$CaCO_3 + MgO + CO_2 = CaO + MgO + 2CO_2 \qquad (2)$$

The calcium oxide CaO in the second equation above is, of course, quick-lime. In accordance with the reactions discussed in previous sections on glass formation the two products of equations (1) and (2), that is, calcium oxide and magnesium oxide, will react with the silica and alumina of any mixture of ceramic-forming materials, such as frits or bodies, so as to produce glasses and fluxing materials. Calcium aluminosilicates, in particular, are important materials in high-temperature bodies and glazes, eg porcelain type bodies.

TABLE 7

FUSING POINTS OF FELDSPAR AND SYENITE

		Initial	Final	Remarks
Potash Feldspar		1160°C	1530°C	Incongruent, sluggish;
Soda Feldspar		1170°C	—	highly viscous melts
Calcium Feldspar		1150°C	—	
Nepheline syenite	Sinters:	1060°C	1200°C	Sharp flux
	Fuses:	1150°C		

Feldspar and china stone

These are aluminosilicates of potassium, calcium and sodium (and also barium). Most ceramic bodies used to make pottery, tiles, porcelain, bone china, earthenware, faience, majolica and others contain a proportion of either feldspar or china (Cornish) stone as the flux. These fluxes are also used in enamels, frits and glasses. Some properties are shown in Table 7.

In the ceramic body the sluggish fusing taking place over a long temperature range, which is a feature of feldspathic, and especially china stone, bodies, means that the potter has adequate control over the firing cycle. Pure glasses (frits) of the same chemical composition would fuse and vitrify the body much more rapidly, converting the mixture of clays, quartz and glass almost instantly into a liquid mass upon the attainment of the maturing (maximum-firing) temperature.

Individual varieties of feldspar are almost never found naturally. They invariably occur as mixtures of the various types. As they were deposited from the parent rock in the form of mixtures of albite and orthoclase, or albite and anorthite, it is to be expected that feldspars used by the potter and glass-maker are mixtures of the main types. This explains their variations in properties and melting behaviour. The potash feldspar used in glass and enamel making, for example, invariably contains some sodium, while soda feldspars contain calcium and potassium.

Since the potter is interested in the glassy properties of feldspar, and particularly the way it flows, a useful and simple test is to place small compacted pellets of ground feldspar on the sloping surface of ceramic trays in a kiln and to examine the resulting flow patterns (see Fig 7). If a comparison is made

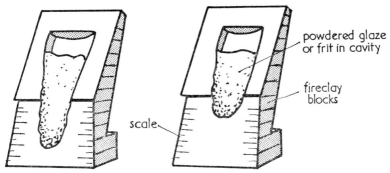

Fig 7   The flow behaviour of molten materials such as glasses, frits and glazes can be compared by allowing small quantities of powder to fuse in the kiln and run down inclined fireclay blocks as shown here. The more fluid in the glass the further it flows

of different feldspars, placing them adjacently on a single multicell test slab, valuable information can be obtained about which material has the sharper fluxing powers, about the fired colour, and the potential strengthening powers of the materials. The length of the journey made by the flowing glass as it melts in the kiln is a measure of the fluxing power. Of course, this is a simple and empirical test, and like all such tests has to be used with caution. Additional information, such as chemical composition, mineralogical composition, and grain-size distribution, about the various samples, makes it possible to obtain a complete picture of the way in which feldspars will behave when blended with other raw materials in the making of ceramic bodies and glasses.

The colour of the fired feldspar, as in most ceramic and glass materials, will be determined by the concentration of iron and titanium present.

China Stones are mixtures of feldspathic minerals and quartz, giving a more sluggish firing behaviour than feldspars. After the last war, Manx stone (see Fluorspar) was also developed for British users as a fluorine-free material, and is now used in other countries, including the USA. The advantages of having a material that will not develop fluorine gases in the kiln are considerable: the kiln linings last very much longer.

Cornish stones are classified as buffstone (considered unsuitable for fine ceramics because of its dark colour); hard purple; mild purple; hard and soft white. Commercial blends now available are usually fluorine-free.

The main variety used in pottery as a flux contains potash feldspar, soda feldspar, mica, quartz, kaolinite and sometimes small amounts of fluorspar, apatite, tourmaline and topaz.

6 WOOD ASHES

These are materials obtained from burning a wide range of vegetable substances: timber, grasses, stalks, cereal husks, etc. Since the ash content, the inorganic constituents, of any vegetable substance is very low, say 0·1 to 3%, the potter needs to burn a lot of vegetation to obtain his ash. The chemical composition of ash, even from the same plant, may show great variations over a period of time, depending on the geographical location of the plant. Between one type of plant and another, the compositional variations are even greater.

The appeal of ashes especially in art ware glazes is that the potter and enameller can obtain unique colouring and textural effects. The minute traces of some rare-earth oxides, or possibly the form of the silica in the ash, may yield a ceramic effect quite unobtainable by controlled chemical reactions with conventional, chemically processed materials. The interpretation of the effects of these ashes on ceramic glazes is very difficult, since frequently the results depend on phenomena that are difficult to detect outside the sophisticated ceramic laboratory using advanced apparatus.

The chemical composition will depend on the geographical location of the plant being burnt. For example, tropical grasses grown on starved soils are found to contain unusually high silica concentrations. Nearer home in Europe and N. America, highly siliceous ashes result when nettles and elder woods are burnt.

Just as clays depend for their compositions on the parent rocks and the rocks over which they have travelled during their deposition, so ashes of plants depend on the soils in which they grow. The plant's chemical constitution is built up by assimilating soluble minerals from the soil. In effect, the plant is acting as a chemical concentrator of selected compounds. Plants may contain all the other main 'ceramic' oxides such as alumina, ferric oxide, phosphates, soda, potassia, calcia, magnesia, titania, and those of manganese and sulphur.

But even more important, perhaps, are the trace elements as boron, cerium, molybdenum and even vanadium. A normal oxide analysis does not indicate their presence, let alone the amounts involved, but they are very important in glazes. The age of the plant also affects the chemical composition of the ashes obtained from it. In trees, for example, the silica content of the bark rises with age. Young, sappy growth will often have much higher concentrations of alkalis than older, toughened branches and stalks. Pruning from apple trees are often used to obtain ash. Their CaO content depends on their age, that from young plants being higher than from old.

7 ALUMINA

Alumina, Al_2O_3, is, of course, not a flux although its behaviour during firing may lead to a reduction in the temperature of a given composition, depending on the amounts present and the nature of the other materials (see below). Alumina is rarely added to bodies, frits or glazes, as the pure compound. It is contributed by clays, feldspars, kaolins and other aluminosilicates, that is, when it is chemically combined with other materials. Although one may discuss separately the effect of alumina on the fired ceramic, it is often misleading to do so. Alumina, with silica, is one of the cornerstones of clay science. In pottery and enamelling it is almost inevitable that where silica is, there also is alumina. Usually alumina is present in much smaller quantities and it is difficult to say simply what its function is. It is common to attribute refractoriness to it: to say alumina increases the fusing point, making a ceramic more difficult to melt. In glaze and enamel making, alumina may tend to reduce the danger of crystallisation.

All this may be valid, but the role of alumina is much more complex than is realised by many craft workers. The subject must be considered in relation to all other substances in the particular mixture being heat treated. The point will be clarified by considering the behaviour of alumina in two cases, as an impurity, and as the main constituent of a body.

As an impurity we find that alumina is present as a minority constituent in silica bricks used to make furnace linings. The alumina impurity comes from the silica rocks used as raw materials in silica brick manufacture. Pure silica, in the form in which it is used in the refractories industry, melts at temperatures above 1700°C. Pure alumina melts at temperatures above 2000°C. However, when these two highly refractory materials are mixed and heated, the fusing points of the mixtures are immediately lowered. Now if only 5% Al_2O_3 is added to the silica, the fusing point of the mix is about 1545°C. Such is the effect of a small amount of alumina on the silica.

When alumina is the principal constituent of the body being fired we find that as the alumina content increases, the fusing point of the system also rises until, at 100% Al_2O_3, a super-refractory material results. Indeed, in the manufacture of firebricks and other refractories, the products are graded according to alumina content. Common firebricks, for instance, contain 35-37% alumina, while high-duty materials contain 60-75% alumina. There are also pure alumina ceramics for special purposes.

Alumina is also contributed to ceramics by bauxite which is the commonest material for making pure alumina. Bauxite is a hydrated alumina, a sedimentary rock with iron oxide, titanium oxide and clay as impurities. Other forms of alumina used in ceramics are diaspore, gibbsite, hydrargillite, sillimanite, kyanite and other aluminous minerals. Most of these are mainly of interest to refractories producers.

8 PIGMENTS AND COLOURS

The raw materials of ceramic colours are the oxides and salts of metals such as cobalt, nickel, manganese, chromium, antimony, selenium, cadmium and vanadium. These colouring oxides can be used to produce attractive ceramics simply by adding them in the required amounts to glazes, enamels and clay bodies. Naturally, care must be taken to see that they are blended thoroughly to give uniform distribution. The firing temperatures and kiln atmospheres (whether reducing or oxidising) will also have a critical effect on the final result.

TABLE 8
COLOURS OBTAINED WITH OXIDES

Metal Oxide	Chemical Symbol	Colours obtained
Chromium	Cr_2O_3	Yellow, green, reds
Cobalt	CoO	Blue
Copper	CuO	Blue, green; red (if reduced)
Iron	Fe_2O_3	Yellow, brown, green
Manganese	MnO	Brown, yellow, purple
Nickel	NiO	Brown, khaki, blue
Vanadium pentoxide	V_2O_5	Yellow, blue, green

Modifying agents

In addition to the basic colouring oxides, the potter and enameller uses certain modifying agents which in themselves do not produce colours but when blended with the colouring oxides or salts will have critical effects on the final colour. To quote a few well-known examples, chromium oxide normally gives greens but when blended with tin oxide, it will produce chromium-tin pink. When a small amount of chromium oxide is fired with alumina at very high temperatures, it is possible to produce a body stain called the chromium-alumina pink. Another example is zinc oxide which, when added to chromium, produces browns instead of greens and zirconium dioxide ZrO_2 makes a fine range of turquoise blues with vanadium oxide.

In industrial potting, body stains, for example, are formulated to suit particular types of body composition, and one particular stain may produce quite a different tint if the body composition is altered. This also applies to glazes and enamels. The firing temperatures will also affect the colour. Indeed some bright pigments are quite unstable at high temperatures and either burn out or are radically altered.

In using any ceramic colour it is important to match the composition of the colour with the firing conditions and ceramic compositions in which it will be used. Table 9 shows some of the effects of various common modifiers and other ceramic raw materials on the colour produced by basic colouring agents.

TABLE 9
EFFECT OF MODIFIERS OR DILUENTS ON COLOURS

Modifier or Diluent	Chemical Symbol	Effects
Alumina	Al_2O_3	Produces pinks with chromium oxide
Silica	SiO_2	Will affect the intensity of the redness of chrome-tin pinks
Lead oxide	PbO	Common flux; makes selenium reds black
Titania	TiO_2	Enhances 'redness' of iron oxide; makes yellows with chromium
Whiting	$CaCO_3$	Makes bright light greens with chromium oxide
Zirconia	ZrO_2	Makes torquoise with vanadium pentoxide
Zircon	$ZrSiO_4$	Stabilises nickel browns

The cheapest colouring oxides are iron, cobalt, chromium, manganese and nickel. These are powerful stains so intense colours can be obtained with very small amounts.

Blending and firing

The commonest method of blending the ingredients of a colour recipe is to weigh out the materials, mix by hand, grind

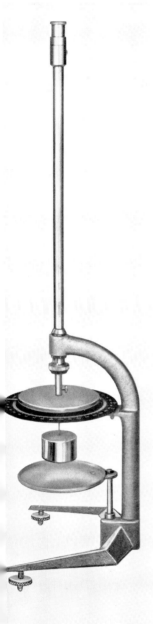

Page 65 *(left)* The torsion viscometer is a simple instrument for measuring the fluidity and viscosity of ceramic slips. The metal cylinder, suspended on wires of different gauge, rotates in the slip, the properties of which can be read off a scale *(courtesy A. Gallenkamp Co Ltd)*; *(above right)* simple metal shapes in copper and other metals can be shaped by hammering them into depressions in wood logs *(courtesy Edward Winter)*

Page 66 Ceramic sculpture is an ancient art and the clay must be in an ideal condition for such delicate workmanship. Here a replica of the statue of Josiah Wedgwood is being made in black basalt body whose colour comes from iron and manganese oxides *(courtesy Wedgwood & Sons Ltd)*

in a mortar and pestle and then sieve through a 40s screen. The colouring material must be uniformly dispersed in the rest of the ingredients before the powder is put into a saggar or other ceramic vessel and fired. When the product has been fired at the temperature required to develop the colour, it is then ground, usually in water, as are glazes. The material is then dried and the resulting powder can be easily crushed and used in the normal way as if obtained from a colour supplier.

During calcination the same sort of reactions occur as in the firing of other ceramic mixtures (see previous sections on silicate science). When the blends of oxides, clays, and fluxes are heated, the chemical reactions leading to certain critical processes take place, and must be governed in the same way as for reactions leading to the formation of biscuit clay wares or glazes.

TABLE 10
FIRING TEMPERATURES OF CERAMIC AND ENAMEL COLOURS

Colours	Calcination Temperature ($°C$)	Temperature of use ($°C$)	Remarks
Antimony Yellows	850-950	Up to 1050	Bleaching and volatilization may occur Rapid firing best
Cadmium-selenium	400-650	Up to 850-900	Rapid fire, glost and enamel only
Chromium Greens	1100-1250	Any	Stable, but Cr_2O_3 may volatilise over 1000°C
Cobalt blues	1100-1350	700-1200	Very stable at all temperatures
Iron colours	560-800 (determines the precise tint)	Up to 950-1000	Very unstable; affected radically by kiln atmosphere and composition of glaze, clay, etc
Manganese Browns	1000-1200	750-1100	Colour depends on modifiers present
Nickel colours	1100-1300	Up to 1150	Unstable; tint alters with environment and temperature; may crystallise
Vanadium colours	750-1300	To 1450	Very stable
Black colours	1100-1350	Depends on composition	Colour depends on environment and temperature; blue, green or brown tint may predominate
Copper colours	850-900	To 950	On-glaze and inglaze enamels only

E

The chief factors in colour preparation for the potter and enameller are the temperatures in the kiln and the kind of atmosphere. Table 10 shows the temperature ranges used for firing some colours in pottery, and some indication of the temperature ranges in which these materials can be used on pottery, in frits and glazes.

Art and studio colours

Certain colouring effects obtainable in enamels and ceramics are of special interest to the craftsman. The industrial producer may have difficulty in obtaining such colours in his 'mechanised' conditions and it is by concentrating on these effects that the artist can give his work distinction from mass-produced ware.

A classic example of such an effect was for many years the reduced copper red colour, known as *rouge flambé*, sacrificial red, or *sang de boeuf*, produced by the ancient Chinese. It is only recently that American ceramists, using the electron microscope, have proved that the effect is due to the presence of metallic copper finely dispersed in the glaze, although this was guessed at many years ago.

Celadon

This term covers a range of coloured glazes beloved of art potters and used by the first Josiah Wedgwood to describe his self-coloured green earthenware. Simply, the colour is due to iron oxide fired in chemically reducing conditions. The effects obtained in practice depend critically on the composition and physical nature of the clay body and glaze, and the firing temperature and soaking time, as well as the gaseous atmosphere.

The amount of iron oxide and the degree of its reduction, that is, its chemical form, in the glaze, are perhaps the two most critical factors on the celadon colour. Art potters make celadons by using 1-4% iron oxide in the glaze, but an analysis of ancient Chinese stoneware celadons suggests that the body itself contained as much as 20% iron oxide. The migration of iron from the body to the glaze must therefore be considered as an important factor in developing this unusual colour.

The colours of celadons have been described in many ways,

usually in the language of the poet. Most potters recognise them as grey-green or grey-blue glazes with varying shading and colour intensity effects showing up as the pot is turned in reflected light.

The materials used to add the iron to the glaze will affect the celadon colours. Pure red iron oxide, Fe_3O_4, bought from chemical suppliers, may yield quite different effects from those obtained with red ochre (as iron-stained clay which may also contain some manganese).

The effect of temperature on the colour of iron oxide may be gauged from Table 11 which shows colours obtainable by calcining copperas, $FeSO_4$.

TABLE 11
EFFECT OF FIRING TEMPERATURE ON THE
COLOUR OF IRON OXIDE

Temperature of Calcination (°C)	Tint of Fired Powder
600	Nasturtium
650	Coral
700	Pillar-box red
800	Purple, red
1000	Violet

These tints are unlikely to be obtained when the iron oxide is fired in a glaze or body, but the information does demonstrate the critical effect of temperature on iron oxide colours. Iron oxide is a very unstable ceramic pigment.

State of oxidation of iron

Iron oxides exist in two common forms, as ferrous (valency of two), FeO, and as ferric (valency of three), Fe_2O_3.

A third oxide is also known, called ferroso-ferric oxide, Fe_3O_4, which exists in nature as magnetite or lodestone. This is more stable than the other two and is a 'compound' oxide similar to Mn_3O_4 and Pb_3O_4. When acid is poured on to the ferroso-ferric oxide, the resulting solution contains a mixture of ferric and ferrous salts.

The iron oxide supplied for use in ceramics is ferric oxide, Fe_2O_3. It occurs naturally in several forms, eg a red haematite (also known as kidney iron-ore because of its distinctive appearance).

The colours of celadon glazes are due to the presence of mixtures of ferrous and ferric oxides. The ferrous oxide contributes blue tints and the ferric oxide contributes the yellow or brown tints. It is wrong to think that by converting all the iron present in the glaze into the ferrous state, FeO, a blue glaze would result. The chemistry of iron-reduced glazes is very complex. Even the colouring behaviour of iron oxides in clay is a matter of argument. For instance, it is not known how lime reduces the staining power of iron oxide in clays (bleaching).

Blue engineering bricks are obtained by firing certain iron-stained clays in reducing atmospheres to convert some of the ferric iron to the ferrous state. Such bricks are usually mechanically very strong.

Copper reds

These are inglaze colour effects due to the presence of finely dispersed metallic copper. The copper compound employed in making these glazes is usually cupric oxide, CuO, added to the raw glaze and fired in a reducing atmosphere to obtain the desired effect. Cupric oxide (black copper oxide) is obtained from chemical suppliers. The essential red-glaze-forming reactions may be represented simply as follows:

$$4CuO \rightarrow 2Cu_2O + O_2 \qquad (1)$$
$$Cu_2O + CO \rightarrow 2Cu + CO_2 \qquad (2)$$

The metallic copper, Cu, is the agent making ceramic glazes red. The type of red colour depends on the amount of copper present and the composition of the glazes. Copper reds are currently being produced in studio and industrial workshops, using $0.4-6\%$ CuO in the starting glaze recipes.

Copper compounds in glazes fired in oxidising conditions normally produce green colours and attractive effects may be obtained by using a firing cycle in which some periods are reducing and other periods oxidising. This technique gives green and red blotches in the ware.

Brongniart, the French ceramist, analysed Chinese red glazes and developed the following recipe for copper reds. It can be used as a starting point for experiments: 76.0% SiO_2, 7.75% Al_2O_3, 6.08% CaO + MgO, 3.72% $K_2O + Na_2O$ and 6.0% CuO. In addition to the glazing techniques of blending copper oxide with raw materials, applying to the ware and firing in reducing conditions, it is also possible to convert plain glazes into copper red glazes by causing the copper to migrate into the glaze from a specially applied clay paste. The refractory clay paste is blended with the copper oxide and smeared on to the glazed and fired article. The whole is dried and then fired in the reducing kiln during which the copper is transferred to the glaze. The paste, which must be refractory and must not vitrify if it is not to stick to the glaze, is broken off to reveal the coloured glaze.

Lustre colours

Preparations made by ceramic suppliers are the usual source of raw material for the art and craft potter although it is possible to obtain pleasing effects by using the original lustre-reduction methods, starting with pastes of clay and pigmentary oxides, similar to the procedure described above for copper reds. With the paste method, copper sulphate, silver nitrate, and bismuth nitrate are commonly used to yield reds, yellows, and mother-of-pearl iridescent effects respectively. The applied pastes carrying these salts must then be reduced during firing.

Modern 'silver' lustres used commercially are based on platinum, a process claimed to have been invented by John Hancock in about 1800 at the Spode factory in England. The secret of this discovery was subsequently maintained by the factory, for a few years at least, by describing the platinum as 'pail gold'.

Lustres are very thin films of metal oxides or metals deposited on glass and ceramics, and their colours are due to the interference of incident and reflected light. They are applied from solutions or suspensions of metallic salts or metallic resinates in specially prepared media, using brushing or spraying. The lustre appears immediately after firing and no polishing or burnishing is required as for certain types of liquid gold.

Table 12 shows the materials for preparing lustres.

The organic constituents, the resins and solvents, used to prepare liquid lustre preparations employed commercially, especially in producing medium priced gift-ware and souvenirs, have a critical effect on the workability and fired properties of lustres.

TABLE 12
MATERIALS FOR PREPARING COLOURED AND
COLOURLESS LUSTRES

Colourless Lustres	Coloured Lustres
Alumina	Iron (red and yellow)
Zinc oxide	Cadmium (yellow)
Lead oxide	Uranium (yellow)
Bismuth oxide (irridescent)	Nickel (brown, gold)
	Cobalt (blue)
	Gold (gold)
	Platinum (silver)

Water as a raw material

Water is one of the essential raw materials for the ceramist and enameller. The type of water, its hardness and content of soluble salts, are very important. Special watch should be kept on any change in the source of supply. Water used for making slips, especially casting slips, should be as pure as possible, and the re-use of water after pressing clay is often an important source of contamination. The gradual build-up of soluble salts in the water may cause serious faults in the casting department (see Section 2).

section 2

SHAPING PROCESSES

9 SHAPING METALS FOR ENAMELLING

Metals for enamelling are shaped by cutting, shearing, bending, hammering and filing. Clays and ceramics are shaped by plastic moulding and by casting suspensions of clay and nonplastics. Because of the vitreous coatings applied to both types of material, however, the design objectives and indeed the principles of designing metal and ceramic articles may be very similar. The need to understand the relationship between glassy coatings and underbody must be considered by both types of craftsman.

Metal shapes for enamelling in industry are made from sheet steel, copper, aluminium and other metals by cutting, stamping, punching, spinning and drawing. Many of these simple shaping methods are suitable for the craft enameller and amateur worker. The simplest technique with which the craft is usually taught is that of cutting out a circle of copper sheet, followed by hammering this disc into a simple bowl using a 'nest' hollowed out of a log of wood. The rough bowl shape is then planished with a metal hammer. This consists in inverting the rough shape on to a steel stake, rounded at the top, and tapping the metal being formed so that its shape is gradually perfected. The effect is not only to give the copper its final shape, but also to enhance its surface finish.

Copper is malleable and ductile and thus easily shaped in the cold state. Shaping by hammering increases its strength and hardness. The amount of hammering on cold steel stakes, as described above, determines the ultimate hardness and strength but it should be noted that prolonged hammering will reduce the ductility, just as the prolonged working of clay in the hands will reduce its plasticity. Excessive cold hammering and planishing of copper may also lead to internal cracks and cause fatigue failure. Once the copper disc has been shaped as described, a foot can be hammered into the bowl and the edges ground smooth on a grinding wheel; plastic-carborundum, or rubber-alumina compositions are used. The article can then be hand polished with steel wool or similar abrasive to finish it.

The most important factor in the satisfactory enamelling of metals is the nature of the bond between the glass skin and the metal base. In order to provide good bonding between the copper and the glass enamel a series of surface preparatory operations must be carried out. Briefly, the metal surface must be cleaned thoroughly, and in such a way as to expose a fresh metal surface to the glass enamel, giving the fusion a chance to marry with the metal in the firing process. Various techniques are used depending on the technique used to shape the metal, the type of metal, and the composition of the enamel (see below). Rubbing the metal with steel wool, followed by polishing with powdered pumice is a common method.

In the case of our simple planished copper bowl described above, there should be very little dirt or grease on the copper. The pickling process designed to clean it up consists simply in immersing it in dilute acid. The solution of acid is made by pouring one part by volume of sulphuric acid into 16 parts by volume of water. This makes a 6% solution.

The copper article must be handled with tongues, of course, when being immersed in the acid solution and the acid should be poured into the water—never water into acid—to avoid dangerous splashing. When the entire copper surface has been swished around in the acid, the article can be removed and rinsed in a bowl of clean cold water to remove all traces of acid. The next step is to apply a coat of adhesive such as gum tragancanth or starch glue (dissolved in water). Another method is to heat the piece to dull red and then wash it in vinegar containing common salt.

Surface effects on all metals employed in vitreous enamelling can be modified by metal working. Of course, if labour and skill have been spent on planishing or chasing (cutting patterns into the surface of the metal with certain small tools specially shaped for the job) it would be illogical to hide the surface effects so made by completely coating the metal with an opaque enamel.

The usual procedure is to enhance the metal by metal-working methods and then to apply transparent enamels which add to the final results by highlighting these surface markings. A wide range of textures can be obtained, especially on copper, in this way.

Etching is a chemical treatment by which areas of metal may be corroded away to form patterns. Areas that must remain unaffected are protected with wax, asphalt or similar protective liquids and waxlike substances. These protective agents are applied to the metal by brush or spray. When the acid is applied, the exposed metal is attacked and eaten away to yield various decorative effects.

TABLE 13
PROPERTIES OF METALS USED FOR ENAMELLING

Metal	Specific Gravity	MP (°C)	Elasticity Modulus* Tension	Torsion	Poisson Ratio
Copper	8·93	1088	16	7×10^6psi	0·35
Aluminium	2·70	660	9·0	3.5×10^6psi	0·34
Sheet Steel	7·9	—	30	11.5×10^6psi	0·29
Cast Iron:					
Grey	6·8-7·2	—	16.5	6.5×10^6psi ⎫	0·25
White	7·7	—	—	⎬	0·28
Silver	10·5	961	11·5	4×10^6psi	0·38
Gold (22C)	17·5	—	11·5	4×10^6psi	0·42

* The tensile modulus of elasticity (Young's Modulus) is the ratio of stress to strain in tension. The shear or torsion modulus is the ratio of the stress to strain in shear or torsion. The Poisson ratio is the ratio of transverse strain to longitudinal strain under load.

The aim in craft enamelling is for the artist to develop skills both in metal working and in vitreous enamelling. By combining the peculiar properties of each, he can produce an effect that may be greater than the sum of the parts. This again is why the craft enameller, like the potter, must understand the limitations and potential of his raw materials.

Soldering of metals may be done with traditional soldering irons or propane hand torches. The soldering iron is really a mild steel spindle with a copper tip and wooden handle. Copper is used for the tip because it easily retains the thin coat of solder, a process known as 'tinning'.

Soldering is the process of joining two pieces of metal or alloys with an alloy that is more soluble than either. Soft solders for common work with sheet steel and containing lead and tin are usually unsuitable for enamelling since they would melt in the enamelling furnace. Various solder compositions are available from hardware and metal suppliers for different metals. Enamellers use hard silver solders and borax fluxes to apply them. High-temperature silver solder is necessary to prevent re-melting in the enamel furnace. Naturally the temperature of the soldering tool must be considerably higher than that of a soldering iron used to solder with soft lead-tin compositions.

The techniques of soldering is invaluable to the vitreous enameller who wishes to make cylinders, vases and other vessels, and also complex structures of many parts. Soldering irons may be heated by naked flame, by gas, or by electricity.

Spinning is a metal shaping method involving the rotation of a blank on a lathe, forcing the metal with rollers into the desired shape. It is used for making complex cylindrical articles such as tall coffee pots and some narrow necked vessels.

A silver solder with a softening point of about 320° contains 97·5% lead, 1% tin and 1·5% silver. By increasing the silver content at the expense of the lead, the fusing point can be gradually increased to the level required in enamelling. Silver solders do not wet the metal as easily as soft solders but with skill it is possible to use them both with corrosive borax fluxes and with resin (non-corrosive) fluxes. A handbook on soldering should be consulted for details of soldering operations, types of fluxes and temperatures.

Welding is a complex technology, using highly sophisticated equipment and processes. Simply, it consists of heating the two metal components to be joined and forcing or beating them together, either with or without a flux. The metal enameller wishing to use welding in building up assemblies of steel sheet, bar and tubing for subsequent glass enamelling should first consult welding engineers for instruction in the skills of welding, especially in regard to safety measures.

Cloisonné. This is a process involving the building up of a network of wire on to the metal surface, each cell then being filled in with glass enamel. The wires keep the molten enamels from running into each other and disturbing the desired effect. The flat wire is bent and shaped into the desired pattern or arrangement, and then temporarily secured to the metal surface, which might be a copper tile or vase, with viscous glue or other suitable medium such as plastic adhesive. A preliminary firing at about 800-820°C secures the wire to the base metal. Then the powdered enamels, slightly wetted or containing a temporary bond such as cellulose derivative (carboxy-methyl cellulose), are compressed by pallette knife or similar tool, into the cells formed by the wires, and the whole object is fired in the usual way. The melting vitreous enamels bond the wires together and onto the metal base. Any organics (glues and temporary bonds) burn out during the first firing. The adhesives should be selected with care so that they leave no traces of carbon which would make the finished article black or smoky.

Metals used to shape the wires in *Cloisonné* include copper, steel and brass; for jewellery and other precious objects made of gold and silver these two noble metals are used for the wire. Since the wires are to be bent and distorted, sometimes repeatedly before they assume their final form, they must be pre-treated by a process known as *annealing*. This involves heating them to red heat and cooling in cold water, followed by the usual technique of immersing in dilute sulphuric acid (other acids are also used, depending on the type of metal) and washing in clean cold water (see above under 'pickling').

Since powdered enamels applied in this way shrink during firing, it is found that several topping-up stages will be necessary, with another firing after each one before the enamel level comes up to the wires. The next process is to grind and polish the surface of the fired and cooled cloisonné to enhance the appearance of the wires and the glass. Grinding removes the gloss and a final firing is needed to restore it.

10 SHAPING CLAY CERAMICS

The success of the shaping process, whether by hand or machine, depends on understanding the effects of pressure and stress on the clay-water system. The more the potter understands the physical and chemical laws governing the behaviour of wet and dry clays, paying close attention to the effects of soluble salts, colloids and nonplastics (for example, sulphates, lignin and quartz respectively), the more readily will he make his material respond to his creative actions.

All the various methods of shaping pottery can be broadly classified into two methods: plastic shaping, and slip casting in plaster moulds.

11 CLAY AND WATER

Water is a raw material. It is rarely found in the pure state. Its effects on processing and on the finished article are as critical as those of the other raw materials. Yet because it is so plentiful and commonly used in everyday living, water is taken for granted.

Given time, water is the universal solvent. Unless he takes the trouble to find out, the potter may believe his water to be pure enough for the job of potting. Frequently, especially if it is well or river water, it contains very high concentrations of dissolved minerals, especially if the river is polluted by industrial effluent. Water is a patient servant. But it has its limits of endurance. In small or moderately sized potteries that fabricate their wares by slip casting in plaster of Paris moulds, the re-use of press water in slips, combined with the use of too much casting scrap, can lead to a gradual and disastrous build-up of soluble salts in the clay.

It is not only dirt and soluble salts that affect water's usefulness to the potter. The weather makes itself obvious when the temperature drops below $0°C$ or $32°F$ by changing liquid into a solid. But long before the extremes of temperature are reached, water alters its properties. This is frequently to such an extent that the potter's slips, glazes and pigment-water mixtures undergo quite marked changes in the workshop.

Hardness in water

Hard water does not readily give a lather with soap. In some areas this may be due to soluble salts in the water in the form of bicarbonates, chlorides, sulphates and nitrates. The salts are usually calcium and magnesium sulphates, chlorides, etc, although sodium and iron salts may also be present.

If only bicarbonates are present in the water its hardness is *temporary*, and is removed by boiling. The heating of such water converts the soluble bicarbonates into insoluble carbonates which are precipitated (come out of solution) and are deposited on the bottom of the vessel as scum—the fur in kettles, for example. *Permanent* hardness (due to the other salts mentioned above) is not so easily removed and must be treated with chemicals.

How water affects clays

The first experience a potter has with clay is when he adds water to it in order to make it plastic for shaping.

By gradually increasing the amount of water added to a given quantity of clay, the potter alters its plastic properties. Eventually the amount of water exceeds a critical level and the resulting slushy viscous mass ceases to retain its shape when pressure is applied by hand. In other words, the clay-water mix is no longer plastic but has become a fluid, or what is known in ceramics as a *slip*.

Slips are suspensions of clay particles, often in the presence of non-plastic particles such as feldspar and quartz, in water.

A distinction should be made between *slips* and *solutions*. Compare, for example, the behaviour of common salt when added to water, with the behaviour of plaster of Paris when it is added to water. The salt is dissolved to form a solution, whereas the plaster of Paris does not dissolve but forms a slip or slurry. (To be precise, some of the plaster does dissolve in the water but only a very small quantity.)

In ceramic slips the bulk of the materials remain undissolved. Clays, feldspars, quartz sands, and other materials such as lead bisilicate frit, whiting, zircon, etc, do not dissolve in the water used to blend them. It is true that in certain conditions tiny amounts of some of these substances will be dissolved by water. Some of the potassium and sodium salts, for example, of feldspar may be dissolved or *leached out* if the feldspar is ground very finely in water. The effects of these small amounts of leached substances may be very important—in altering the fluidity and thickening properties of the slips, for example.

Most materials used in pottery are slightly soluble in water and the degree of solubility may be increased by certain pro-

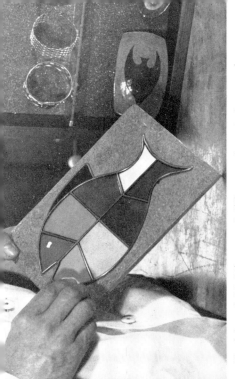

Page 83 (above left) Mixtures of different coloured clays can be used to make 'marble' finishes. Here brooch blanks are being cut from plastic clay for making ceramic jewellery; (above right) after firing. enamels are polished to restore the brilliance of the glass. Here an enamel mosaic of a multicoloured fish is being polished; (left) enamel cloisonné is a highly skilled technique with which simple as well as complex designs can be made. The enamels are built up inside carefully placed wires, and the whole fired to give a strong structure (courtesy Podmore)

Page 84 *(above)* Clay articles can be shaped by pressing plastic clay into plaster or pitcher moulds. The simple shape shown here was formed in a pitcher mould with a palette knife for embellishing a Wedgwood vase. Similar but more complex moulding methods were once used to make early Staffordshire figures *(courtesy Wedgwood & Sons Ltd)*; *(below)* a modern de-airing pugmill in which the air is removed from plastic clay for moulding. Note the pressure gauge and the homogeneous structure of the extruded clay *(courtesy Thomas-Porzellan-Werke)*

cesses: increasing the temperature of the water may increase the solubility; adding another salt may alter the solubility, and so on.

The most dramatic illustration of the effect of soluble salts on clays is given, perhaps, by the effects of small quantities of sodium silicate (water glass) on the flowing and thickening properties (fluidity and thixotropy) of clay-water slips. The effect is known as deflocculation and is considered under *Slip Casting*.

Plasticity

Plasticity is often closely related to other properties such as the shrinkage and distortion of claywares during drying and firing. So some grasp of these relationships should help the potter to produce fault-free ware from a certain type of material.

The following factors affect the plasticity of clay and ceramic bodies: 1. Particle size and shape. 2. Air entrapment or removal. 3. Rate of strain, ie the speed of working the clay on the wheel and the amount of pressure applied. Faster working reduces cracking dangers. 4. Soluble salts, especially those acting as deflocculents, that is, agents that cause a clay-water slip to flow more easily without the addition of more water (see below under *Casting Slips*). These processes are discussed in more detail in the section on iron exchange below. 5. Ageing or souring. 6. Surface tension which may be altered by adding certain agents.

Discussion

Clays, consisting of aluminosilicates and other minerals that have been ground very finely by transportation, as for instance in the formation of sedimentary clays, are usually much more plastic than clays that have not been so ground, eg primary kaolins. Ultrafine particles are called *colloids*, and the matter is then said to be in the colloidal state. Colloid science started with the discovery that some substances which appear to be in solution would not pass through membranes such as cellulose film and parchment. These substances therefore are considered to be in a different physical state, which is called the colloidal state.

F

Many substances can be obtained in the colloidal state, including some that can also be dissolved in water (crystalloids) and caused to pass through membranes. In other words it is not the substances themselves that are called colloids or crystalloids, but the state they are in. Simply, colloids are particles whose size comes between the size of particles of solute (the substance being dissolved) in true solutions, and the larger sizes of suspensions or slips. Colloidal particles measure between 10^{-5}cm and 10^{-7}cm (that is, from 0·0001mm to 0·000001 mm).

Very small amounts of colloidal matter in a clay-water suspension may have a marked effect on that system. For example, to keep heavy lead frits and other non-plastics in suspension in glazes, it is possible to use 0·1-0·5% of bentonite, a clay that contains a very high proportion of colloidal material.

The plasticity of clays has also been called the 'life' of pottery. Once fired, clay loses its plasticity and is unworkable as a plastic material. This has caused many potters to relate plasticity to the organic content of clay, and it is a fact that clays high in organic matter such as lignin and other carbonaceous material are often very plastic. The effects of these organic materials is complicated and cannot be ascribed merely to their fine particle size—the fact that they are often colloidal.

For example, the ageing or souring of some clays will often induce a rise in their plasticity. The effect has been attributed to the chemical action of the organic acids formed when the organic content of the clays decomposes. Such acids tend to flocculate (coagulate) the particles of clay and thus improve the plasticity (see below).

Artificial plasticisers

Potters often add materials to their clays and bodies in an attempt to improve the plasticity. Vinegar is a common agent. In making non-clay ceramics, such as in the fabrication of oxides that have no natural plasticity, it is often essential to add such an agent to make possible a fabricating technique. The properties of some ceramics suffer in the presence of clay and it is then desirable to replace natural clay by man-made plasticisers.

A rough idea of the *mechanism of plasticity* in natural clays can be obtained by considering how an artificial plasticiser, such as glycerine, will act as a lubricant in the movement of particles of non-plastics. The particles of say alumina, milled finely, will move relative to each other when they can do so on the thin films of glycerine (Fig 8). The particles are held

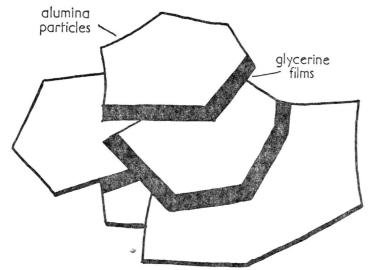

Fig 8 Glycerine films act as a lubricant for the sliding of particles of alumina or other nonplastic grains, conferring 'pseudo'-plasticity on the material

together to make a pseudoplastic mass by the surface tension of the viscous liquid.

Taking the above idea a stage further, consider a system in which finely ground grog (fired clay which has no plasticity) is mixed with a small amount of clay slip. The clay slip lubricates the grog particles and confers workability on the whole mass, but in a much more complex manner than the glycerine-alumina combination mentioned above.

Cellulose compounds

Compounds such as carboxymethyl cellulose, which have high molecular weights, long-chain molecules, and give very viscous solutions (similar to colloidal systems in behaviour) are now being used in ceramics for plasticising some materials where clay is undesirable. The craft potter and enameller may find them useful in other sections of the craft, in glaze and enamel slip stabilisation and for making glaze films hard before firing, for instance. Other artificial plasticisers are tannates, quebracho extracts, alginates (from seaweed), and wax emulsions. The action of some of these is discussed in other sections of this book (eg on *Casting Slips*), and glaze or enamel slips.

Particle-size distribution

Any potter's clay or other raw material prepared for use in a body, glaze or enamel, that is, in the powdered state, upon analysis is found to consist of groups of particles of different grain sizes. Simply, a cupful of powdered clay may be compared with a cupful of mixed marbles, beans, peas, rice grains, sand, sugar, pepper—right down to grains that are invisible. The way in which these various size groups are put together is called their particle-size distribution.

It is important to note that natural clays or milled materials such as feldspar, sand or whiting do not consist of grains of the same size (the particles in the cup are not all peas, or all rice grains) but that there is invariably a mixture of sizes.

Highly plastic clays such as ball clays cannot be used alone to make pottery because they would twist out of shape on being dried. It is usual to modify the overall grain-size distribution by adding some larger particles, eg ground grog, feldspar, and flint.

Particle shape

The importance of the particle shape of clays on their plasticity can be understood by noting the behaviour of a collection of marbles and that of small chippings of slate. The way in which the slate chips, when lubricated with glycerine, move over each other with a sliding action, compared with the sluggish rolling action of the marbles gives a very rough idea of the different types of behaviour of non-plastic and plastic materials respectively (eg ground quartz compared with clays).

Kaolinitic clays owe their plastic properties to the particle shape of these clays. However, other clay minerals have differ-

ent particle shapes and may be also highly plastic. Halloysite
has particles in the form of cylinders or rolled parchment. The
manner in which halloysite scrolls pack together and cause
shrinkage during drying, and then suddenly collapse during
firing, is quite distinct from the drying, shrinking and firing
behaviour of kaolinite.

The particle shape of clays and non-plastics in pottery bodies
is also important for another reason: the behaviour of clays in
working (throwing, coiling, and casting etc) depends, as already stated, on the presence of soluble salts. The large surface
areas offered by the kaolinite platelets to the absorption of
such salts (see below under ion exchange) play an important
role in clay-water systems, not only in developing plasticity
but in conferring casting-slip stability.

Electron-microscopic studies have shown that other clay
minerals such as, for instance, illite and montmorillonite (the
latter is the essential ingredient of bentonite clays mentioned
above) have particle shapes distinct from kaolinite and halloysite, so the subject is more complex than merely observing the
difference between spheres and platelets.

Rate of strain

This was mentioned above as affecting plasticity. Potters
used to working on the wheel with a variety of clays will know
that the force applied to the spinning clay by the fingers affects
the ways in which the clay can be shaped. They may also learn
by trial and error that the speed at which they can press, knead
and work the clay (that is, the rate of strain) will determine
how the finished clay article behaves. In other words, if cracking is to be avoided there is usually an optimum rate of strain
to be used in shaping the pot.

A certain amount of work has to be done on a lump of
plastic clay before the pot evolves. On the wheel it is best to do
that work as fast as possible and use the highest rate of strain,
so as to produce a pot inherently free of cracks. A slowly moving
wheel and laborious, deliberate hand manipulations usually
fail to produce the desired results on the potter's wheel, and in
the end the clay breaks up when only slight deformations are
applied.

Air entrapment

This is another important problem in producing plastic bodies. In the pottery industry, of course, plastic clay is invariably passed through a vacuum pugmill to extract the air. Many craft potters use small pugmills (Fig 9). All potters need to

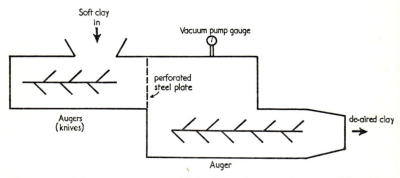

Fig 9   De-airing vacuum pugmill for blending and homogenising plastic clays. Simple workshop models are available as well as large industrial units. If the vacuum chamber is excluded, the clay leaving the mill is not free of air

understand the effects of trapped air in clay. Wedging clay, ie cutting it in half and throwing it together repeatedly in such a way as to expel the air, is a common learner's exercise in potting, and the effectiveness of wedging usually decides the usefulness of the pots thrown from such clay. The way in which de-airing of clays appears to improve their workability is not fully understood but it certainly improves the texture and cohesiveness, yielding a better throwing body, and giving less loss on fabricating machines.

12 SOLUBLE SALTS

Ion exchange has been mentioned as influencing plasticity. This topic is very important in understanding the behaviour of all clay-water systems, but particularly so in clay slips and casting slips, so its treatment will be reserved for the following section on *Casting Slips*. However, it can be stated here that soluble chemical compounds such as acids, sulphates and chlorides, which tend to make the particles of clay stick together and form flocs (ie those that flocculate the clays) do improve the plasticity of many clays. On the other hand soluble salts such as soda ash and sodium silicate which tend to force the particles of clay apart (ie disperse them) adversely affect the plasticity. The way in which these agents produce these effects is described below.

At the beginning of this section it was mentioned that small amounts of soluble salts are very important in regard to the properties of clays. The texture of fabricated and dried bodies may be critically affected by such agents. For example, if acids are used to flocculate and improve the workability of a clay the resulting flocs, ie large aggregates of particles, tend to make the structure more 'open' and permeable to water. Because it is more porous the dried clayware may be much weaker mechanically than a clay not treated with acid or other flocculating chemical. So, the potter tempted to improve plasticity by adding acids such as vinegar or hydrochloric acid, should take care not to impair the green strength of his products too much.

13 METHODS OF PLASTIC SHAPING

The craft potter uses a wide variety of shaping methods. Some of these are: 1. Pinching from a ball of clay. 2. Coiling. 3. Slab-forming and building. 4. Basket weaving. 5. Pressing in moulds. 6. Throwing on a wheel.

Different methods of forming may require different types of body in terms of plasticity and water content. Usually, since the craft potter is using his personal skills to work and shape the clay, his knowledge of how water and plasticity affect his results will be obtained by trial and error. However, it is worth noting that if the same clay body is being used in, say, a large workshop, with several potters using different forming methods, it may be necessary to modify the consistency of the clay.

The clay for pressing in moulds would need to be fairly soft and it would not have to support itself once the shape had been formed by pressing the clay against the inside surface of the mould, since the plaster of Paris would do the supporting. Furthermore, the drying of the clay would start almost at once as the plaster began to suck up the clay's water. This would make the clay article more rigid and prevent distortion. On the other hand, an article to be shaped by a free forming method such as coiling or throwing would need clays that are much stiffer and able to support their own weight to prevent slumping.

Texture of clay bodies

The texture or 'feel' of clay bodies prepared for shaping either by hand or machine is an important property. It affects the finish of the clay articles, the mechanical strength, the development of faults such as cracks, pinholes, blebs and stresses in the ware and the behaviour of the body in firing.

Texture depends on the following factors: 1. The fineness of grinding of the ingredients, and hence the particle-size distribution. 2. The particle shape of the various ingredients. 3. The hardness of the various materials. 4. The solids and water ratio. 5. The degree of deflocculation or dispersion of the particles. 6. The content of air.

Highly plastic clays are usually unfit for shaping without the addition of some non-plastic such as grog or flint (quartz). In using such clays the potter, by experiment, adds varying amounts (weighed out and recorded) of milled grog (chamotte) or similar material, the effect of which is to open up the dense, plastic clay, and to make it less prone to distortion and cracking as it dries. Grogs or chamottes, are fired clay or used materials such as saggars, kiln furniture and similar spent refractories, that have been crushed and milled into the desired grain-size distribution.

Bodies which contain grog dry more quickly than all-clay bodies. However, each clay has an optimum amount of grog for which it will produce the necessary workability. Beyond that limit the body loses its plasticity, dries quickly in the hands, and starts to crumble.

Use of grogs (chamottes) in bodies

Many craft potters use grogs as a means of altering the texture of their clays and to keep the body straight during drying and firing. There are two important factors of potter's grogs. First, there is porosity, which depends on the chemical composition of the raw materials used to make the grog, and the firing temperature. If the clays used to make the grog contain a lot of flux during firing, high percentages of glassy material will be formed, and the grogs will be glassy and not so porous, as when refractory clays are used. Second, there is the grain-size distribution, that is, its fineness or coarseness. In low-temperature bodies, the grog may remain in the clay body solely as an inert filler, without reacting with the clay and fluxes and without fusing very much. However, as the firing temperature rises, the grog is acted on by the clay and fluxes and, in the case of some low-melting grogs used in high-temperature bodies, the particles of grog may be dissolved by the vitrifying clay, yielding a very strong and well-bonded vitrified ceramic.

Highly porous grogs that have been made from refractory clays at low firing temperatures will obviously soak up a lot of water when wetted. During mixing with clay and water, these spongy grogs will absorb much more water than would be required to obtain the same workability with the use of clay bodies alone.

TABLE 14

TYPICAL SCREEN CHECK ON MILLED GROG

Residue retained on 40s sieve		2·5%
„ „ „ 60s „		14·6%
„ „ „ 120s „		10·9%
„ „ „ 150s „		50·1%
„ passed through 150s sieve		21·9%
Total		100·0%

Simple vibratory sieving assemblies can be obtained for screening. For very fine materials, such as ball-milled flint or glaze, more sophisticated methods are used but a rough idea of the grinding efficiency can be obtained, even with ball-milled materials, simply by washing a pint or other suitable volume of ground slop material (after first weighing it, of course) through a 200s mesh sieve and drying and weighing the residue.

As a rough guide, grogs for general use contain maximum grain sizes of 3-4mm diameter and about 45% particles measuring less than 0·5mm in diameter. The type of mill used to grind grog affects the type of grain-size distribution.

Textures of plastic and cast bodies

Many potteries produce ware by hand-shaping and by casting from slips. They find that the porosity of the green ware made by plastic shaping is often quite different from the porosity of cast ware. (Cast ware when fired in ordinary kilns is invariably more porous than plastic shaped ware, providing the firing temperatures and heat cycles are the same.) Providing the two bodies are made from the same raw materials with the same grain-size distributions, to the same recipe, the cast ware is normally less porous (that is, it is less absorbent to water) than the plastic shaped articles. The difference may be seen from Table 15.

TABLE 15
POROSITY VALUES OF CAST AND PLASTIC SHAPED WARE
OVER A PERIOD OF WEEKS

	Porosity (%)				
Cast Jugs and Plaques	27·1	28·0	28·1	27·5	27·0
Hand-moulded Vases and Bowls	34·0	34·9	35·0	34·6	33·8

The higher the porosity the less 'dense' the clay ware and the more water it will absorb. The property is important if glaze is applied to green ware.

It is seen that the difference in porosity between cast and plastic shaped ware (for the above article) is about 7%. The effect is due to the use of chemical agents in the casting slip (see below under *Casting*).

How texture of green ware affects fired body

The manner in which pottery is shaped and moulded has a critical effect on the texture or structure of the body. In turn, this will affect the behaviour of the clay in the firing process.

The conclusions of detailed examinations of the above processes may be stated as follows:

(1) Cast bodies usually have a more dispersed structure than plastic shaped ware. This provides faster vitrification and sintering in the kiln. Cast ware therefore would be fully vitrified at lower temperatures than plastic shaped. (It should be noted of course than in practice earthenware is not fully vitrified.)

(2) The fired size of pots made by slip casting and subsequently fully vitrified will be greater than identical ware made by plastic moulding and fully vitrified.

(3) Cast ware is less prone to distortion and warping in the kiln when vitrified than moulded ware.

Particle alignment

The manner in which the particles of a clay or clay body (including the non-plastic) line up or are orientated, during shaping by plastic methods or casting, is very important for subsequent drying and firing. When the particles begin to move in the body, due to shrinkage in the heat processing, the way in which the particles line up has an important effect on

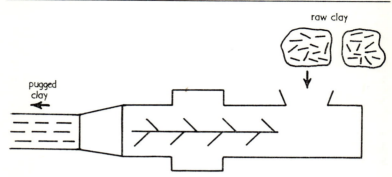

Fig 10 Particle alignment in kneaded clay. Raw clay added to a pug-mill may have its particles randomised. After passing through the pugmill, its particles are lined up as shown. Similar realignment may occur when clays are shaped by throwing

the final results (Fig 10). For example, in throwing a pot the base of the article obviously does not receive the same degree of working with the fingers as do the walls of the pot. This usually results in some difference in the shrinkage of the walls and the base, leading to cracking of the latter. The skilled thrower usually compensates for this by applying extra pressure to the base in forming. Particle orientation is also critical in causing variations in density and porosity in different parts of the article. It can be very important in casting large items since with some slips segregation of the heavier particles occurs in the slip, and this means for example that the feldspars and other non-plastic fluxes tend to segregate and are deposited at the bottom of the mould during casting. When these articles are fired, the sections containing the higher proportions of fluxes will vitrify earlier than those sections that are made up of flux-free body. This must be taken into account in compiling casting slips and also in fabricating by plastic methods.

14 CHEMISTRY OF CASTING SLIPS

Even for the potter determined not to be 'corrupted' by the use of casting slips, there is much to learn about the property of clay-water mixtures from a study of the behaviour of such slips. The water content of a casting slip made from earthenware body (ball clays, kaolins, flint and feldspar) and deflocculated with alkalis may be only slightly higher than the moisture content of a plastic clay prepared for throwing or coiling. The caster is really working with liquidised clay.

Preparing casting slips

Before the principles of chemical deflocculation were understood ceramic shapes were often cast in plaster moulds simply by mixing clay with water and pouring the slip into the mould. When the required thickness of the article had been built up, the excess was poured off and the article allowed to dry before being removed. The plaster of Paris mould extracted the water from the slip by suction, leaving the thin skin of clay cast onto the inside of the mould. The process is roughly similar to what happens when a container of syrup is emptied: a thin film of viscous liquid remains on the bottom and walls of the container. Of course, with the use of porous moulds such as plaster, the process is accelerated because of the extraction of water from the clay-water slip.

With the above simple method, the clay slip contains a large amount of water (about 15oz of water in each pint of clay slip if the pint weight is 28oz). There were two important consequences of this: 1. The moulds soon became saturated with water and clogged up, thereby ceasing to suck up water from the clay slip poured into them. 2. The thickness of the castings was low and the resulting article therefore weak.

Early potters using this technique knew that if they could increase the amount of clay in a given volume of slip (that is, make a pint of it weigh more) without making the slip too viscous, thus preventing it from being poured into and out of the moulds, both of the above problems would be alleviated. There would then be less water entering the mould and the walls of the casting would be thickened because of the higher density (mass in unit volume) of the slip.

The discovery that certain chemical compounds, when added to the clay-water mix in small amounts, would produce the desired result meant the birth of a new fabrication technique in the ceramics industry, leading to the large-scale mass production of all sorts of complicated shapes previously mouldable only by great manual skill and the expenditure of much time.

The essential difference between the alkaline casting slip, one treated with chemicals to make it flow more easily, and slips not so treated is one of bulk density (pint weight, or gram/litre, etc). In British and American practice, for instance, a pint of alkaline casting slip weighs about 36oz. On the Continent we would say that it has a bulk density of 1·8 gram/cm³. Without the chemicals (deflocculents) the pint weight would be only 28oz (1·4g/cm³) for a slip of comparable pourability (fluidity).

Deflocculents

The small quantities of chemicals added to the clay and water in preparing alkaline casting slips are called deflocculents and the resulting effect is one of deflocculation. It is essentially a process of dispersing the coagulated or agglomerated particles within the clay-water system.

In the natural state and when blunged with water, plastic clays are usually made up of aggregates or flocs, that is, even after prolonged mechanical stirring and beating in water, the clay particles are not fully dispersed. Inside these flocs there is always a certain amount of bound water. Simply, the clay particles, in clinging together in small groups, trap films of water inside these groups. Now if some way is found to disperse the groups (flocs) one immediate effect is to release the bound water into the slip (Fig 11).

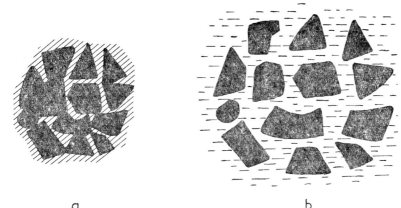

a   b

Fig 11 (left) Flocs of clay particles showing the enclosed 'bound'
water; *(right)* the dispersing effect when the clay particles are separated by adding chemical agents such as sodium silicate

This in turn increases the volume of the slip slightly (we
now have more than a pint) and the slip flows more easily,
being less viscous. We say that the slip's *viscosity* has been
reduced. The term viscosity is a measure of the thickness or
sluggishness of slips and other liquids.

TABLE 16
WATER CONTENTS AND DENSITIES OF SLIP AND CLAYS

Type of Slip	Pint Weight (bulk density)	Water Content of Slip (%)
Clay and Water (no chemical)	28oz (1·4gm/cm³)	50%
Alkaline Casting	36oz (1·8gm/cm³)	25%

When the clay particles are separated as described above,
the films of water released into the slip undergo a change in
density, since it is known that the density of the bound water
in clay flocs is higher than the ordinary water in the slip (by
about 40%). This explains why there is an increase in the
volume of the pint of slip with which we started.

Now the question is: how do we cause the particles of clay
in the flocs to separate? In other words how do we bring about
deflocculation? If we can separate the particles and make them

move about in the slip, it should be possible to make the slip flow more readily, and it can then be used for casting pottery in plaster moulds. The answer is: we use chemical agents known as deflocculents.

Chemicals used as deflocculents

The two commonest compounds used to deflocculate clay slips are sodium carbonate (known also as soda ash) with the formula Na_2CO_3, and sodium silicate (known also as water glass) with the formula $Na_2O.SiO_2$ (more strictly $Na_2O.nSiO_2$ since the ratio of soda to silica in the material may be varied considerably—see below).

Soda ash is a white crystalline powder that must be kept dry, since it absorbs moisture from the atmosphere, and the product may then be similar to common washing soda with a variable amount of water of crystallization. When a given quantity of such a damp material is added to the slip it will be difficult to say precisely how much soda ash is going into the mix and how much water.

The second compound used to deflocculate slips is a viscous transparent greyish liquid usually stored in airtight metal drums. It can be added to the slip either by weight or by volume (recipes once fixed by experiment must be maintained, of course). Sodium silicate is very adhesive and is also used for making various types of cements, for instance, in the refractories industry.

Tannates, such as sodium tannate, are also used in casting slips mainly when the plastic clay content is low or when the slip is known to be short of colloidal matter. The tannic acid formed in the slips helps to provide protective colloids, stabilising the properties of the slips.

Use of deflocculents

Before adding deflocculents to his clay-water mixtures for casting the potter needs to determine the correct amounts. This is important because 1. Very small amounts are needed. 2. Too much chemical causes thickening—the opposite of the desired effect. 3. Excess chemical additives may cause production troubles such as scumming on the ware, crawling of the glaze, unglazed patches on glost ware, as well as casting difficulties such as ropy slips and wreathing (see below).

In an industrial earthenware body consisting of ball clays, kaolins and feldspar, the total amount of deflocculent, that is, soda ash and sodium silicate combined, is about 0.25-0.35% of the dry weight of the clay. An example would be that 100 kilograms of dry clay need about 250gm of deflocculent, or 220lb of clay needs $8\frac{1}{2}$oz of deflocculent.

If a solution of soda ash and sodium silicate is made up using equal parts of each (a ratio of $1:1$ and using water) it should be possible to calculate the weight of combined deflocculent present in a certain volume of solution (for example, a pint or a millilitre). By adding increasing amounts of this solution to a batch of clays (with blunging) we find that the fluidity of the slip so formed alters in a special way. At first there will be little or no effect then, with increasing deflocculent addition, the clay-water mix will begin to flow more easily, until with a certain optimum amount of deflocculent a very fluid slip is obtained.

The action of the chemical solution has been to break up the flocs in the clay causing the particles to repel each other by means of electrical charges developed through the mechanism of deflocculation and make the slip thin and fluid. Of course, a small amount of water is also added to the clay slip when the solution of chemicals is added and this must be taken into account in any precise measurements, since as we already know the pint weight (that is, the amount of water in the clay) has an important effect on the viscosity of the slip.

Reverse effects

If we continue to add the solution of soda ash and silicate to the slip the action is eventually to thicken the slip again. Thus, it is important not to add too much chemical. For most clay bodies containing a high proportion of plastic clays, the turning point does not come suddenly. In fact, it is usually possible to add quite an excessive amount of deflocculent beyond the optimum point before we note any thickening up of the slip.

Some indication of the behaviour of clay slips when deflocculated can be obtained from Fig 12.

Most technical reports on the theory and practice of alkaline casting slips show graphs plotting viscosity versus the amount

G

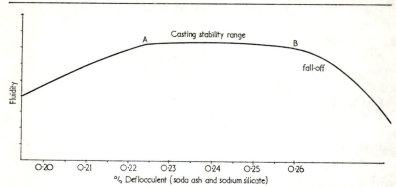

Fig 12 Curve produced when increasing amounts of deflocculent such as soda ash and silicate are added to clay-water mixtures. See text for explanation

of deflocculent. In this case the curves obtained are upside down (see Fig 13).

In Fig 13, the curve for slip treated with soda ash alone indicates that there is not so much leeway or waiting time as with sodium silicate. In other words, silicate is a much gentler deflocculent. However, for various technical reasons, to obtain a stable slip that will store well, it is best to use a combination of ash and silicate.

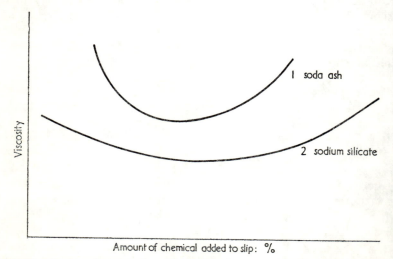

Fig 13 Curves showing the change in viscosity (thickening power) of casting slips treated with deflocculents of different types: (1) soda ash with sharp deflocculating effect, and (2) sodium silicate with its gentler action

15 ION EXCHANGE

Previous sections have emphasized the importance of dissolved salts and other substances in the forming of ceramics. Small amounts of salts in clay bodies, slips, glazes and enamels may have a disproportionately large effect on the properties. The phenomenon of ion exchange (base exchange, cation exchange, and anion exchange are related terms) is important in understanding the behaviour of clays. I have already mentioned that ion exchange affects plasticity. It is also part of the mechanism responsible for casting slips' behaviour and the way in which glaze and enamel slips can be thickened up to improve their application to pottery or metals.

Ions in solutions

When a salt is dissolved in water it can be assumed to split up into parts, called ions. The ion may carry a positive or negative charge. Thus, when sodium hydroxide (caustic soda) is dissolved in water we may represents its behaviour as:

$$NaOH \rightleftarrows Na^+ + OH^-$$

The sodium ion Na^+ carries a positive electrical charge and is called a *cation* (because if electrolysed it would move towards the *cat*hode in the electrolysis bath); the hydroxyl ion, OH^-, carries a negative charge and is called the *anion*, because it would move towards the *an*ode if electrolysed.

It was mentioned above that the effect of adding alkalis such as soda ash and sodium silicate was to deflocculate the slip. The ions formed in solution by these agents are not simply found by splitting up the molecule. In fact a process known as hydrolysis occurs in the case of sodium carbonate, and we obtain equations:

$$(1) \quad Na_2CO_3 = 2Na^+ + CO_3''$$
$$(2) \quad H_2O = H^+ + OH'$$
$$(3) \quad H_2CO_3 = 2H^+ + CO_3''$$

The overall effect of this is to remove the hydrogen ions (which make the system acidic) through combination with the CO_3'', ions to yield carbonic acid H_2CO_3; and the most important result for clay deflocculation—leaving a preponderance of hydroxyl ions in solutions.

The fact that the above simple addition of soda ash to clays makes the clay-water mix alkaline gives us the name *alkaline* casting slips. In general, acids flocculate or coagulate slips, whereas alkalis deflocculate them, although some potters find that additions of soda ash make clays more plastic (usually acid treatment is recommended as a plasticity improver).

From these remarks on ions, electrical charges, and also reference previously to the particle shapes of clays, we now see that the properties of clay-water mixtures depend on phenomena that are far from simple.

For our present purpose, we can assume that the plasticity and fluidity of clay-water mixes depend on the ions present. By altering the types of ions present, it is possible to modify the properties of ceramic suspensions. Furthermore, many physical properties of clay slips are governed by the electrical and other forces between the particles and between the ions in the water and those particles.

Now, ions can exist inside the crystal of the clay mineral as well as in the water of the slip. It used to be thought that the ions playing the most important role in clay-water systems remained on the surfaces of the particles, but this was probably oversimplifying the problem. The way in which ions exchange places in the clay mineral and in the solution is of vital importance to ceramics technology. Positive and negative ions can pass between liquid and solid, and continuously do so, which means the process is not static but dynamic.

To quote one simple example of the practical importance of ion exchange to the potter we may refer to deflocculation. When hydroxyl ions OH' (this may also be written OH⁻) are made to form in a slip by the addition of soda ash, as described above, the negative charges of the OH' become attached to the clay particles, replacing other ions such as H, Na, and K.

Simple because *'like charges repel each other'*, the negatively charged clay particles push each other away, thus breaking up the flocs or aggregates, leading to thinning of the slip (a reduction in its viscosity).

Thickening of casting slip

If too much alkali is added to the slip it begins to thicken. Briefly, what happens is that the dispersed particles again lump together and in doing so recapture some of the water that was previously released upon deflocculation. Since the slip is deprived of water (free water) and as the flocs are forming we note a thickening effect. The process is complicated and it is known that several effects take place simultaneously. The thickness of the films of water and the aura of ions around the clay particles, the nature of the changes, and the concentration of ions all have an influence.

Practical aspects of casting slip preparation

1. The casting slip fluidity must be controlled so that it will flow easily into the narrowest sections of the mould without beginning to gel while the mould is being filled.
2. The water content of the slip should be as low as possible in order to prolong the mould life and to speed up the process.
3. The non-plastic constituents, eg grains of feldspar and quartz, should not settle out, that is, the slip should be stable. This is achieved by correct selection of plastic and non-plastic materials, proper grain-size distribution and adding the optimum amount of deflocculent.
4. The amount of deflocculent used is normally less than the amount needed to give the slip maximum fluidity. In other words, a slight increase of deflocculent to a real casting slip used in practice should lead to a slight thinning of the slip and certainly not to thickening. If thickening does ensue, it indicates that too much deflocculent has been already added to the clay and water in preparing the slip in the first place.
5. For a given body composition try to keep the pint weight (bulk density) and the amount of deflocculent constant from day to day. This procedure should keep the fluidity

and other casting properties of the slip fairly steady. If faults develop the source can be looked for elsewhere. A record of measurements on the slip should be kept. The use of a simple laboratory instrument known as a *torsion viscometer* (see page 65) is invaluable in controlling casting slips.

Self-thickening of slips (thixotropy)

If left undisturbed a casting slip will thicken on its own. This effect is typical of most clay-water systems, glazes and enamels, and is considered to be due to spontaneous structure formation within the slips. This thixotropic effect is used in the casting of ceramics, and for certain articles it is necessary to control it in narrow limits (only on an industrial scale, however). If the thickened slip is agitated or stirred its previous fluid state is resumed.

Using the above-mentioned torsion viscometer the potter can check two important properties of his slip: the fluidity and the thixotropy.

Together with the pint weight (bulk density) these two measurements will provide a thorough daily check on the consistency or otherwise of ceramic casting slips. The instrument is also used to control enamel and glaze slips.

Some faults in casting slips

As mentioned above sodium carbonate has a different deflocculating effect from that obtained with water glass. The fluidity range with soda ash is much shorter and so mistakes with, or over-zealous use of, ash will have an immediate effect. Soda ash is rarely ever used alone in ordinary casting slips because it produces flabby, unstable casts that do not hold together in the moulds. This agent also tends to yield air-filled casts, causing pinholing and cracking.

On the other hand, if water glass is used alone the drying cast becomes brittle and is difficult to fettle and cut. Another fault with sodium silicate used alone is that it gives ropy, liverish casts, and the slip may be prone to wreathing, a fault that shows up as ring marks on the sides of the articles being cast (see below).

The ratio of soda ash to sodium silicate is obviously important in view of the different effects produced by each. In general, low-plasticity bodies such as those used in making bone china and other porcelains and also some vitreous bodies which rely for their glassiness on high flux contents (as opposed to high firing) need more sodium silicate than ash. For instance the ratio for bone china may be three of silicate and one of ash.

Sodium silicate is sold in various grades. The ratio of the Na_2O and SiO_2 in the compound varies. The potter should therefore discover which type of sodium silicate is being supplied and ensure that the supply is not altered without his knowledge. Possible grades are $Na_2O.SiO_2$, $Na_2O.2SiO_2$, $Na_2O.3SiO_2$ and $Na_2O.4SiO_2$.

Effect of plaster in casting slips

In potteries which use plastic moulding methods such as throwing or mechanical shaping all scrap clay obtained in the casting shop can be used up for plastic moulding. However, when casting is the only method of fabrication, as in many small commercial potteries producing for the giftware and souvenir trade, the problem of what to do with the casting scrap may become serious.

When plaster moulds are filled with slip, the slip is contaminated with plaster of Paris ($CaSO_4$) from the moulds.

The operator has to cut rims and scrap is produced. If this scrap is thrown away, the economics of the pottery suffer; if it is re-used to make casting slip, the gradual build-up of calcium sulphate in the slip may lead to production problems. Again it comes back to the subject of ions and their effects on clay-water systems (see previous sections).

Alkalis, we have seen, deflocculate slips. Acids and some salts tend to flocculate them. Plaster of Paris is a flocculent and, since it is partly soluble in water, small quantities soon get into the casting slip. Re-used again and again, casting scrap may contribute so much sulphate to the slip that an increasing amount of alkali has to be added in order to achieve the original fluidity. Eventually the slip will become overloaded with chemicals and prove to be quite unstable and unsuitable for casting (faults include flabbiness, ropiness, wreathing, and failure to solidify in the mould).

Jelly formation in slip

This fault is known as 'livering' because the surface looks like wet liver. The fault may be due to air in the slip and to its having been left standing too long; excessive use of sodium silicate; plaster in the slip; hard water, or the presence of soluble salts from any other source.

Small holes (pinholes)

This fault may be due to the slip or the moulds, or both. All steps must be taken to prevent air entering the slip. Hot moulds or excessively dry moulds may cause pinholing because they suck up water rapidly causing air entrapment.

Bad slip drainage

This usually appears in the form of ridges on the insides or outsides of the cast hollow ware. A similar fault is known on thrown articles caused by uneven pressure in shaping. The concentrations of deflocculent should be checked. Ridges on the outside of hollow cast ware may form when the slip casts up very quickly. The first 'layer of slip' poured into the mould starts to solidify before the subsequent layer has been poured in. One solution to the problem is to spin the mould on a turntable. If this fails to cure it, the fault may be due to variation in mould porosity, causing some parts to absorb water more rapidly than others.

Dry glaze patches

If, after the ware has been glazed, some areas are dry and not covered by the glaze, the fault may be traced back to the casting process. The unglazed patches may be less porous (ie more highly vitrified) than the rest of the article. When the glaze is applied by dipping, these 'hard spots' refuse to suck up the glaze, and show up 'dry' in firing.

The fault is also prevalent in colour spraying on biscuit articles. One theory for this fault (known as 'flashing' and hard spots) is that if the casting slip is allowed to come into contact with the mould too forcefully, the constituents of the slip segregate, leaving patches of clay that have too high a flux content. In other words, the composition of the article is uneven over the surface of the ware, and in firing this unevenness is fixed, thus affecting subsequent glazing.

Drain casting and solid casting

Holloware and other articles such as figures are usually drain cast: the mould is filled with slip, and after the desired wall thickness has built up, the moulds are inverted to allow the excess slip to drain off into containers for re-use.

Solid casting is used for making cup handles and other articles with small cross sections. The two processes are illustrated in Fig 14.

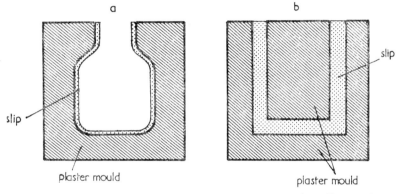

Fig 14 The important difference between drain casting *(left)*, when the liquid clay is left until the required thickness is built up on the mould wall, and the surplus is then poured out of the mould, and solid casting *(right)*, when the slip is allowed to solidify

section 3

MAKING GLAZES AND ENAMELS

16 CHEMISTRY OF GLASSES

The glass films applied to metals as vitreous enamels, and to pottery and ceramics as glazes, are very similar in physical appearance and chemical composition. Whatever difference there is between the two types of glass coating is due to the dissimilarity between the bases to which they are applied.

Glazes and metal enamels are made from the same raw materials. They have the same structures. They are formed by heat treatment and in chemical composition they are made up of various forms of aluminosilicates. Furthermore, one of the main purposes of these glassy films, that of enhancing the appearance of the objects that carry them, is achieved in both cases by the same pigments and stains—ceramic colours.

If glazes and vitreous enamels can fairly be described as being forms of glass, the question arises: What is glass?

An understanding of the simple properties of glass-forming materials such as the fusing points and the principal oxides that they introduce to a glass will help the craftsman in making glazes and frits for enamels. Since the permutations of materials and quantities are so numerous, the task of producing a suitable glass film for a given clay or metal from the whole range of materials available, would be almost impossible on a purely trial and error basis.

Empirically and theoretically the glass maker starts with silica (most glazes and enamel frits contain at least 50% SiO_2). He then lowers the fusing point of silica by adding fluxes such as soda, potassia, calcium oxide, magnesia, lead and boric oxides. Since the fusion point of glazes and frits is not the only important property that must be controlled, it is essential to consider how the above fluxes affect the hardness, the thermal expansion, the crystallisation capacity and the resistance to acids such as vinegar; and also their chemical resistance to alkalis such as detergents. For glazes, the effect on lead solubility is of the utmost importance. Obviously, it is useless making a fusible glass to apply as a glaze or enamel if the fired hard skin cracks or is attacked by food acids when the ware is used.

Thus, by balancing the adverse effects of one substance by the use of another substance, it is possible to arrive at a recipe that, when blended and fired, will cover the pottery or metal with a continuous, stable, hard and durable coating of glass. The simplest approach, perhaps, to understanding glass chemistry is to study the properties of each of the materials used in glassmaking. Another approach is to examine the fired product from the aspect of the final properties and ask such questions as:

1. Which chemical compounds can be used to give the glaze or enamel certain properties, eg crazing resistance?
2. What is the relationship between the glass film and the underbody (the metal or clay), and how is this relationship modified so that glass and underbody can coexist in harmony?
3. What is the difference between the structure or texture of the glass film and the underbody?
4. How do glass films bond themselves to metal or clay bodies?

The practical approach in this book is to describe the effects of the various glaze-making substances in terms of their physical, visible effects. What makes a glass melt? What happens if potassia makes an enamel expand more than the metal? Only when the craftsman can think in these terms and comes to associate, say, alumina with anti-crystallisation, or silica with high-temperature resistance, or lead with high gloss, is it possible to begin thinking of Şeger formulae and 'making the bases add up to one'.

Let us therefore begin by taking a look at common window glass (a milk bottle will do just as well). Briefly, the sand, lime and soda ash are weighed out, mixed and melted in a furnace. The fluxes melt first and lower the softening point of the sand, which is normally a very heat-resistant material. Upon the attainment of a high enough temperature, the liquid mass resulting from this glass-melting process becomes transparent.

If it is cooled fast enough this important property of *trans-parency* is retained. If cooling is too slow, some of the silicates that were formed by the sand and the fluxes (calcium oxide is a flux), instead of remaining dissolved in the glass in the same way as salt is dissolved in water, may come out of solution and crystallise. The glass obtained is no longer fully transparent. Instead of a glass structure, we have one that is partly crystalline.

To oversimplify, the difference between a fast cooled, clear glass and a slowly cooled, crystalline melt is the same as the difference between a glaze and a pottery body. The glaze is composed of relatively fusible materials, heated to form a glassy film that is usually intended to remain transparent. The body on the other hand contains, in addition to a certain amount of flux material, a much larger proportion of non-fluxing materials. During the firing of the body, some of the non-fluxing materials may be dissolved by the fluxes, later to be crystallised out upon cooling. For instance, mullite, an important constituent of many high-temperature bodies, is formed when the kaolinite molecule decomposes in firing. The mullite is crystallised owing to the decomposition and the general melting processes.

The behaviour of glass in melting and cooling offer important lessons for the potter and enameller. For example, some pottery glazes need to be transparent; others are deliberately formulated to make crystals form in them as a means of decoration. The important questions are: Which materials make crystals appear? and What is the effect of temperature and cooling?

Glasses and glazes

From the above we see that glazes and enamel frits are essentially glasses. It is true that there may be wide differences of composition in the many glazes and enamels used for various types of pottery and for various metals such as steel, copper and aluminium. However, they are all glasses in the sense that they are made from silica and fluxes that have been melted at relatively high temperatures.

In fact glaze making for pottery has been looked upon by some ceramists as simply a matter of altering the composition of window glass so as to make it soften and flow without adversely affecting its durability. In fact, it is possible to crush up bottles or window panes, grind them finely into a slip, and dip pottery into the resulting material. Providing the temperatures in the kiln match the fusing point of the glass, the pottery so treated would leave the kiln with some kind of glaze on it. However, it is most unlikely that such a glaze would satisfy the requirements of ceramic glazes in all of the following respects:

1. Pottery glazes must cover the ware with a continuous, impervious coating of glassy material.
2. They should be hard and scratch resistant.
3. They should hold on to the clay body after firing so as not to crack or peel off.
4. They should be decorative and enhance the appearance of the ware.
5. They should resist the attack or dissolving action of the acids and alkalis with which they come into contact during use.

Glazes and enamels exist as films or skins on pottery or metal. Window glass and bottles exist of themselves. Thus, in one very important respect, glazes and enamels are distinct from glasses since some of the properties of glasses in the thin-film state are not possessed by 'bulk' glasses such as a bottle. The potter must always examine glazes in relation to their co-existence with clay; the enameller with metals.

Glasses and enamels

Much of the above reasoning applies also to metal enamels. Window glass could be modified to make metal enamels. Usually the window glass composition would be too refractory, that is, would have too high a melting point for application to metals and it would be necessary to add fluxes. The essential difference between a glass skin for pottery and one for metal is one of thermal expansion. Since metals expand much more during heating and cooling than pottery, the recipes of enamels must be adjusted to take this into account. In the same way certain decorating paints, such as liquid gold and platinum used in ceramics must be modified for use on metal enamels to compensate for the different expansion values.

The essential properties of metal enamels are:
1. They must adhere to the metal in a hard continuous film without cracking or peeling.
2. They must be impervious to liquids.
3. They should be decorative and enhance the appearance of the metal.
4. They must be scratch resistant and durable.
5. They must withstand chemical attack from acids and alkalis and other agents with which they come into contact during service.

Pottery glazes

Bought glazes

Glazes bought from ceramic suppliers are ready for use on the types of clay bodies specified by the supplier. A wide range is available so that a glaze suitable for any body and firing cycle can normally be provided. The customary procedure is for the potter to send a sample of his clay body (or biscuit ware) together with details of his kiln and firing cycle to the glaze manufacturer who then suggests suitable glazes, and possibly a firing cycle, maximum temperature, soaking times, etc.

Prepared glazes can be modified by adding colouring agents, opacifiers and even matte-inducing additives. Experiments along these lines may teach the student a great deal and will point to the general principles of glaze chemistry. Eventually, of course, the artist or the craftsman with aspirations to achieve unique results will investigate new glaze compositions. It is then that he must have a sound knowledge of glaze chemistry.

Lead in glazes

Indeed he may need such knowledge in order to modify bought glazes, for indiscriminate alterations of properly balanced glazes may produce faults in fired glazes, the most dangerous of all being that of rendering the lead soluble. Many low-temperature and medium fire glazes for earthenware and red-clay bodies are built up of two frits (glasses) and small amounts of kaolin and feldspar. For example, a glaze may be made of 60% by weight of borax frit, 30% by weight of lead bisilicate frit and, 10% by weight of china clay. This is a simple recipe and by altering the ratios of ingredients it is pos-

H

sible to alter the fusing and other properties of the glaze. But the raw lead oxide used to make the lead bisilicate glass or frit mentioned in the above recipe is a toxic substance. One of the reasons for making a glass from the lead in the first place was to make the lead harmless.

The process know as fritting is similar to that used to make glass described above. Sand, lead and a little china clay (to contribute about 2-3% alumina) are blended and melted in a furnace to make a glass, which is then poured out into cold water to granulate it. This frit is known as lead bisilicate frit and has the approximate formula $PbO.2SiO_2$, which indicates that one molecule of lead oxide has combined with two molecules of silica (see below). Other ratios of PbO and SiO_2 are possible.

Lead glazes are brilliant, highly craze-resistant, and if properly fritted are absolutely safe in use.

Converting raw lead compounds (white lead is another such material) into glasses by fritting makes the lead insoluble, providing that when such glasses are used in glazes and enamels nothing is done to make the lead soluble again and therefore dangerous. Fritting makes the lead insoluble and safe. But if too much lead frit is added to a glaze or if certain compounds (such as manganese oxide or copper oxide) are added to the lead glaze indiscriminately, the lead may become unstable, that is, soluble and unsafe. Thus, glazes containing soluble lead when used on ware for cooking and serving food may have their lead leached out by food acids, especially vinegar and fruit juices. The consumer may contract lead poisoning.

Borax frits are made by melting borax, silica, whiting, feldspar and some kaolin to give a *borosilicate glass*. Borax and boric acid, the raw materials used to contribute boric oxide, B_2O_3, to glazes and enamels are water-soluble and so have to be converted into glasses before being used in glazes. Now if raw lead and borax were fritted together with other glass-making ingredients such as sand, feldspar and whiting, the lead would become unsafe for the reasons mentioned. The difficulty is overcome by making two separate frits, one containing borax and the other the lead, and then blending with some china clay and feldspar to produce the glaze.

Frits are not used in all pottery glazes; some glazes are made from raw materials, blended, applied to the pottery, and fired, so that the fritting or glass-forming process is done directly on the ware. Nevertheless, the reactions of fritting are common to both types of glaze.

Natural glazes

Some raw materials may be suitable as glazes with only slight alterations in their chemical composition. A simple fusion test (made by grinding and fusing a sample in a biscuit cup) will indicate the fired appearance. If the natural glaze fuses well, producing a smooth glossy coat and pleasing colour and texture, but is susceptible to crazing, it may be necessary to add some silica to the glaze (or to alter the body's expansion). If the glaze is not quite mature, i.e., if it is matte or still contains gas bubbles on the surface, it may be necessary to add a flux such as soda or potash.

Ideally of course, in addition to a knowledge of the physical behaviour of natural glaze materials, the potter should possess a chemical analysis. In this way, he may be able to use the material as a starting point from which to prepare a glaze, using a chemical formula.

Let us trace the procedure step by step through which this could be done. The potter has discovered a source of material that fuses at his firing temperature (say about 1000°C). When ground up, sieved and melted in a small biscuit bowl (coated with milled flint or china clay to prevent it running through the porous container in firing) the material is glassy, transparent and has an attractive colour, or is colourless. It is free of iron blisters and other sources of gross contamination.

A complete chemical analysis is made on the raw material— a costly process and one that must be done by a qualified silicate analyst. This indicates the chemical elements present in the material, usually in the form of oxides; SiO_2, Al_2O_3, Fe_2O_3, MgO, CaO, Na_2O, K_2O, TiO_2, SO_3, and the loss on ignition. The last term refers to the weight lost by the material when it is ignited, that is, heated to a temperature of about 1000°C. The loss is composed of water, organic matter, and carbon dioxide and other gases that are chemically combined with the minerals of the sample.

From the chemical analysis, the potter can now predict some

of the behaviour patterns of the material. By comparing the analysis with those of other raw materials whose properties are well known, it is possible to decide roughly whether the unknown material is likely to be a flux, or a refractory; whether it will be clean or iron stained; and also to predict other ceramic properties. But, most important, it is possible to calculate how much of the material will be needed to contribute a certain quality of a certain oxide, silica for instance, to the final glaze recipe.

This is really the basic principle of making glazes by chemical formulae. If the analyses of the raw materials are unknown, the desired results are obtained after only repeated experimentation. Frequently it is not possible to make a glaze material match certain conditions by trial and error. Complete analyses would have made this clear and saved time and effort.

If all the materials to be used in glaze-making have been analysed, it is possible by simple chemical principles and arithmetic to calculate the amounts of each material to be added to the mixture in order to prepare the glaze and all this before any glazes are actually mixed and fired (see Appendix 1).

Molecular formulae

In practice a ceramist wishing to prepare a new glaze either mixes raw materials by trial and error, or he uses a glaze formula, taken perhaps from the literature. An example of such a formula, known as the Seger formula, is:

$$\left. \begin{array}{l} 0.6 \ PbO \\ 0.3 \ CaO \\ 0.1 \ Na_2O \end{array} \right\} \qquad 0.18 \ Al_2O_3 \qquad 2.0 \ SiO_2$$

The first point to note is that '0·6 PbO' does not mean 0·6 per cent of lead oxide. The above formula is a molecular or Seger formula, named after Hermann Seger, the German ceramist who devised the method.

The purpose of quoting glaze formulae in this form is to make it easy to compare glazes that are made from very different raw materials. Theoretically, a glaze made in ancient China, if represented accurately in the Seger form, can be reproduced with modern materials and methods. In practice, the analyses on which the Seger formulae are based are sometimes slightly inaccurate (they may ignore the presence of tiny amounts of trace elements, for example) and these inaccuracies lead to differences in the original glaze and the copy.

The potter must first decide which raw materials are needed to contribute lead oxide (PbO), calcium oxide (CaO), sodium oxide (Na_2O), alumina (Al_2O_3), and finally silica (SiO_2). In other words all these oxides must be present in the recipe and in the final glaze when it is applied. From the chemical analyses of his available raw materials, the potter can determine whether they are capable of providing all the oxides mentioned in the formula. Obviously if one of the raw materials contains an oxide not mentioned in the molecular formula (for instance, MgO) then that raw material cannot be used for this particular glaze. Furthermore, some raw materials contribute more than one oxide (china clay, for example, contributes alumina and silica), and so they must all be balanced in order that only the oxides given in the formula are present in the fired glaze and no others.

The use of frits (glasses) in glaze and enamel making was mentioned above. Let us use a simple frit formula to illustrate the above principles. Lead bisilicate frit has the molecular (Seger) formula $PbO.2SiO_2$. This formula means that it contains a molecule of lead oxide and two molecules of silica. Now, chemical symbols such as Pb, O, Si, etc stand for a certain definite weight of the element. Thus, Pb stands for 207 parts by weight of lead, O stands for 16 parts of weight by oxygen. Hence PbO (by addition) stands for 223 parts by weight of lead oxide.

The figure 223 is called the 'molecular weight' of PbO. The molecular weight of all other compounds can be so calculated. One merely adds up the atomic weights, found by referring to tables printed in chemistry books and in the appendices of this book. Here are some other examples:

Sodium Carbonate (Na_2CO_3). This contains two atoms of sodium, one of carbon and three of oxygen, giving $(2 \times 23) + (12) + (3 \times 16) = 46 + 12 + 48 = 106$. Therefore the molecular weight of Na_2CO_3 is 106.

Silica (SiO_2). There is one atom of silicon and two atoms of oxygen, giving $28 + (2 \times 16) = 60$. Therefore the molecular weight of SiO_2 is 60.

In the frit, whose formula is given above as $PbO.2SiO_2$, we need to combine appropriate raw materials in such a way as to give one molecule (i.e. 223 parts by weight) of lead oxide, and two molecules (that is, $(2 \times 60) = 120$ parts by weight) of silica. We see therefore that the molecular formula treated in this way will give us a recipe in everyday parts-by-weight terms. For example:

Lead oxide PbO	223 ounces
Silica (sand) SiO_2	120 ounces

However, should the Seger formula specify for instance 0·6 PbO, the 'parts by weight' answer is found by multiplying the 0·6 by the molecular weight of the lead, i.e. $0·6 \times 223 = 133·8$ parts by weight. And so on, right through the list of oxides quoted in the molecular formula. Thus, Parts by Weight = Molecular Part x Molecular Weight.

The arithmetic manipulation of glaze formula using analyses of raw materials and the above principles is a very valuable tool for the potter and enameller and every effort should be made to understand these principles as outlined in Appendix 1.

17 EFFECTS OF OXIDES ON FRITS AND ENAMELS

Basic oxides

The basic oxides in ceramic technology are the alkalis (Na_2O, K_2O, Li_2O) and alkaline earth oxides (CaO, MgO, SrO) and also lead oxide. In writing a molecular formula, the bases are written first as a column, and their molecular parts are made to add up to one (unity), for example:

$$
\left.
\begin{array}{ll}
0.6 & PbO \\
0.3 & CaO \\
0.1 & Na_2O \\
\end{array}
\right\}
$$
$$
\overline{1.0}
$$

This is merely to facilitate comparison between glazes.

The action of the bases is to reduce the fusing temperature of the silica that forms the framework of all pottery glazes and enamels, by fluxing the silica to form fusible silicates (see Section 1). The bases also combine with boric oxide to produce fusible borates. Thus, if soda is heated with silica, the product is a fusible *sodium silicate*. If calcium oxide is fused with borax, the product is a fusible calcium borate. Usually more than two elements are present, and the products are complex silicates, borates, aluminosilicates, and aluminoborates, etc.

The effect of alkalis such as potash, soda and lithia is to raise the thermal expansion of the glass. Unless carefully controlled, the alkalis may raise the expansion so much that the glass film (the glaze or enamel) crazes on the underbody because it does not fit well onto the latter.

Thus, in selecting a combination of bases to flux the silica in glaze making, we must reach a compromise and not exceed a safe limit for alkali concentration. Alkalis also reduce the chemical resistance of glazes if used excessively.

The 'bases' column of a molecular formula may consist of six or seven oxides, for example:

0·3	PbO
0·2	CaO
0·1	Na₂O
0·1	K₂O
0·1	Li₂O
0·1	MgO
0·1	SrO

In fact, especially for alkaline earths (CaO, MgO), the more oxides present the more readily the bases flux the silica in the glaze. In other words, a mixture of bases is better than a single base and the more complex the mixture of bases, the more readily it fuses. This has nothing to do with the actual amount of the bases, but only the number of different bases present. Thus, it is sometimes possible to make a glaze or frit more fusible at a given firing temperature simply by replacing a given molecular part of one base by the same molecular part, using two or three bases. For example:

0·6 PbO	could be made	0·6 PbO
0·2 K₂O	more fusible by	0·1 K₂O
0·2 CaO	converting to:	0·1 Na₂O
		0·1 CaO
		0·1 MgO

Glazes very high in alkalis fuse very easily and because of their high thermal expansion craze easily, forming a network of cracks all over the fired and cooled glaze—an effect that is sometimes deliberately encouraged as a form of decoration known as *'crackle'*. If the network of cracks is rubbed with a colouring oxide, followed by re-firing, it is possible to make a multicoloured cracklé glaze.

Sources of alkalis

The alkalis such as soda and potassia (and less commonly lithia) are obtained from certain raw materials which may be either soluble or insoluble in water. If the sources are soluble it is necessary to make a frit (glass) by melting them with silica and other glass-forming ingredients before the soda or potassia can be used in the glaze. Fritting renders water-soluble compounds insoluble.

Table 17 shows the various compounds used to contribute alkalis and alkaline earths to glazes.

TABLE 17

Alkali / Alkaline Earth	Source (Raw Material)	Formula	Soluble / Insoluble in Water
Soda, Na_2O	Soda Ash	Na_2CO_3	Soluble
	Washing Soda	$Na_2CO_3.10H_2O$	,,
	Sodium Nitrate	Na_2NO_3	,,
	Borax	$Na_2B_4O_7.10H_2O$	,,
	Soda Feldspar	$Na_2O.Al_2O_3.6SiO_2$	Insoluble
Potassia, K_2O	Potassium Carbonate	K_2CO_3	Soluble
	Potassium Nitrate	KNO_3	,,
	Potash Feldspar	$K_2O.Al_2O_3.6SiO_2$	Insoluble
Lithia, Li_2O	Lithium Carbonate	Li_2CO_3	Soluble
Calcium oxide	Whiting	$CaCO_3$	Insoluble
	Fluorspar	CaF_2	,,
Magnesia	Magnesium Carbonate	$MgCO_3$	,,
	Dolomite	$MgCO_3.CaCO_3$	,,
Strontium oxide	Strontium Carbonate	$SrCO_3$	,,

Zinc oxide, ZnO, is also included with the bases in molecular formulae. It may act as a flux but is usually added to achieve special effects such as matteness.

Acid oxides

The term 'acid' used to describe silica and boric oxide in glazes stems from the simple chemical concept that an acid will react with a base to produce a salt. In ceramics the product (that is the 'salt') is usually a complex silicate that has little or no resemblance to the salt produced in a simple chemical reaction of the acid + base = salt + water type, for example:

$$HCl + NaOH = NaCl + H_2O$$
$$Acid + Base = Salt + Water$$

However, in molecular formulae used to describe ceramic glazes, the silica and boric oxide constituents are called acids. Together with the neutral (amphoteric) constituent, the acids now join the bases to give a complete molecular formula, for example:

Bases	Amphoteric	Acids
PbO		
CaO ⎫	Al_2O_3 ⎫	⎧ SiO_2
Na_2O ⎬	Fe_2O_3 ⎭	⎨ B_2O_3
etc. ⎭		

The form is convenient not only for comparison, as mentioned above, but also because it provides the framework for a series of rules governing the formulation of glazes. For instance, for most earthenware glazes fired at 980-1100°C, the ratios of bases to acids in the molecular formula varies from 1:1 to 1:3. For high-temperature stoneware glazes and for porcelain glazes that are once fired, the acid proportion (SiO_2) would rise to about 1:4 or 1:5. The ratio of the total molecules of Al_2O_2 and bases to the molecules of acid should be less than 0·5 in lead glazes if the lead is to be insoluble.

Thus, by using these simple rules, it is possible to obtain information about the firing behaviour of a glaze merely by examining its molecular formula.

Silica is of course the framework of all ceramic glazes and metal enamels. It is the 'body' of the glaze and provides chemical resistance and strength. It is added as quartz sand, flint, and with other materials such as clays, feldspars, nepheline syenite, etc. The form of the silica used, that is, crystalline cryptocrystalline, or in chemical combination, is sometimes important in glass formation as it most certainly is in body formation (see Section 4).

Boric oxide, B_2O, is added to glazes and frits as borax, boric acid and boron minerals such as calcium borate (see Section 1).

Boric oxide is a flux and the borax is one of the two main frits in many industrial low-solubility glazes (the other being the lead frit). It lowers the thermal expansion of glazes, improves the brilliance, prevents devitrification and increases the crazing resistance. Since borax and boric acids are soluble in water they must be fritted with silica and other ingredients to make insoluble glasses. The compositions of borax frits are usually more complex than lead bisilicate, since the former contain a greater number of bases. For example a borax frit may be given as:

$$\left.\begin{array}{ll} 0\cdot29 & Na_2O \\ 0\cdot11 & K_2O \\ 0\cdot60 & CaO \end{array}\right\} \qquad 0\cdot14 \quad Al_2O_3 \qquad \left\{\begin{array}{ll} 2\cdot0 & SiO_2 \\ 0\cdot58 & B_2O_3 \end{array}\right.$$

A boric glaze, developed for firing at about 1000°C on to red clay for pottery, has the following Seger formula, indicating how the bases may be combined to give a low-fusing material even without the use of lead:

$$\left.\begin{array}{ll} 0\cdot786 & CaO \\ 0\cdot011 & MgO \\ 0\cdot080 & Na_2O \\ 0\cdot123 & K_2O \end{array}\right\} \qquad \left\{\begin{array}{ll} 0\cdot154 & Al_2O_3 \\ 0\cdot025 & Fe_2O_3 \end{array}\right. \qquad \left\{\begin{array}{ll} 1\cdot878 & SiO_2 \\ 0\cdot210 & B_2O_3 \end{array}\right.$$

Neutral oxides (Amphoteric)

Alumina in glazes

Alumina is invariably present in glazes and frits, often performing a stabilising role that is noticed only when the amount is varied. In the structure of aluminosilicates which make up many ceramic materials including glasses and frits, alumina prevents devitrification, forming a barrier to the re-ordering of the silica into that state called crystalline.

A small amount of china clay is also added to most lead bisilicate frits in order to contribute some alumina which helps to prevent the lead becoming soluble when used in ceramic glazes. Alumina is added to glazes with clays, feldspars, and other minerals. It is a 'neutral' oxide in relation to the bases and acids discussed above.

Alumina, Al_2O_3, is a highly refractory material. The net effect of adding it to a glaze would probably be to raise its fusing point. If a glaze becomes excessively 'soft' owing to the kiln temperature having to be raised, for other reasons, or if blistering is a problem in a glaze, an addition of alumina, either as such, or as kaolin, may help to harden the glaze and reduce the fault. Alumina improves the mechanical hardness and scratch resistance of glazes. It is important to balance the amount of Al_2O_3 in relation to the other constituents.

Iron oxide, Fe_2O_3, is a flux and a colourant in glazes. The colour depends on the concentration and also on the quality of titania present with the iron, since the latter enhances the staining power of iron oxides. Glazes high in iron oxides may be made to precipitate iron compounds to form crystalline glazes. *Lead oxide* was discussed above.

Other oxides and their effects on frits

Coloured glazes are made by adding transition metal oxides such as cobalt, chromium, nickel, etc. Opacified glazes are made by adding zirconia and tin oxide. Crystalline effects are produced by causing the glaze to precipitate fine or coarse crystals—processes that depend on the rate of cooling as well as the chemical composition.

Strontium oxide, SrO, is a base and has an action similar to PbO. Strontium glazes are usually low in calcium because the latter readily causes crystallisation. In British and American practice, strontium glazes have not successfully competed with lead. However, in certain other countries, such as the Soviet Union, strontium glazes are now commonly used, and lead is a rare constituent of domestic ceramic glazes. Strontium is usually added to glaze batches as the carbonate, $SrCO_3$, in the same way as calcium carbonate.

Zinc oxide, ZnO, is used mainly for stoneware and fireclay bodies and also as a crystallising agent (see: Crystalline glazes).

Titanium dioxide, TiO_2, is used as an opacifier in enamels and as a cream stain (with iron oxide) in glazes. It is usually present in small amounts in clays and other natural materials. The well known 'rutile' breakup effect in crystalline glazes, used for tiles and decorative ceramics, is due to the precipitation of rutile (one of the mineral forms of TiO_2) upon cooling. It gives spangled crystalline effects.

Tin oxide, SnO_2, was once the best and only opacifier for white opaque glazes. Its high cost has now caused it to be replaced by zirconia and zircon. However, tin oxide is a very rich creamy opacifier, without the clinical whiteness of zirconia, and many artists still prefer to use it in spite of the expense. Tin oxide makes glazes very sluggish and refractory, and this should be borne in mind when an opaque glass is made simply by adding tin oxide to clear glazes. The effect will be to increase the firing temperature of the glaze and, if the temperatures in the kiln are not modified, the result may be the production of immature glazes. Tin oxide is not fritted, but is added to the mill, or simply blended with the liquid glaze. Fritted tin glazes would be less powerfully opacified than non-fritted owing to the formation of soluble stannates, which have less opacifying, that is, covering, power than the raw tin oxide.

Zirconia and zirconium Silicate (ZrO_2, $ZrSiO_4$), are used as opacifiers in many white and coloured glazes. Zircon is a very useful material in ceramics because its crystal is highly stable. It forms the basis of many high-temperature stable stains, such as turquoise, greens and yellows, usually in combination with vanadium. When properly constituted, zircon opacified glazes can replace most, if not all, traditional tin glazes. Early failures of some potters to achieve this economical substitution were probably due to ignorance of the precise action of the opacifier. Tin oxide does not behave in the same way as zirconia. Sound practice is to use zircon frits instead of simply adding milled zirconia or zirconium silicate to the glaze. The particle size of the zirconia and zircon is very important, a careful balance of the two being required for optimum results.

Natural glaze materials

The earth's crust contains certain glassy minerals that may be used as glazes with slight modification. These include volcanic ashes, tuffs, obsidians, andesites, pumice sands and perlites. These invariably show a great variation in composition from place to place; their behaviour depends on their mode of formation and other factors such as particle-size distribution and shape, the types of contamination and the way they are used. Each deposit must be treated separately and potters who wish to use them should make tests similar to those described earlier in this section.

18 CLASSIFICATION OF GLAZES

The non-technical potter may be confused by the terms used to describe glazes. A logical classification is difficult to deduce since there is too much overlapping for clarity. Some classifications previously developed include 1. Raw or fritted. 2. Lead or leadless. 3. Crystalline, including matte, vellum and opaque, and 4. Coloured, which may contain one or all of the above three classes.

The above classes of glaze make some implied reference to the chemical composition. For instance, raw glazes may contain relatively high proportions of carbonates such as whiting, $CaCO_3$, as a means of introducing the flux CaO. In fritted glazes the calcium oxide will be present in a frit, a glass that has been pre-fused in order to render the ingredients insoluble.

The classes of 'lead' and 'leadless' glazes speak for themselves. Leadless glazes may either rely on other bases such as a combination of soda, potash, calcia and magnesia for their fusibility, or they may contain boric oxide to provide fusible borates. Since lead volatilises at temperatures above 1180°C it cannot be used in glazes designed for high-temperature firing such as stoneware. It is then necessary to rely on feldspathic type glazes, those made by adding fluxes such as soda or whiting to a feldspar base. The ancient Chinese had a simple glaze-making technique: they ground some feldspar very finely and used that. Their high firing temperatures ensured its melting and produced very strong glazes that married well with the body.

Glazes and bodies

Another method of classifying glazes is that which refers to the type of body carrying them, namely 1. High fire or porcelain types, maturing at 1200-1410°C. 2. Medium fire or earthenware types, fired at 1000-1150°C (this includes most red clay bodies). 3. Low-fire or majolica, fired below 1000°C.

Obviously the chemical composition will affect the firing temperatures and the raw materials must be selected to provide glasses that, when applied or fired onto the ware, will not fuse excessively at the particular firing temperature but will mature enough to provide the desired effects of continuity, imperviousness, durability and chemical resistance.

19   TYPES OF GLAZES

The characteristics of a glaze are determined by its chemical composition, the firing temperature, the type of body on to which it is applied, and sometimes by the cooling cycle. In the latter case, if cooling is done slowly, the glaze may have a crystalline finish, if fast, a glassy finish.

1 Clear white glazes

The thin films of glass formed by applying this type to the ware either in the clay or biscuit state, are usually transparent, free of bubbles, blisters and unmolten raw materials. Bubbles may be present in high-fired ware. The colour and texture of the body can be seen through the glaze and should therefore be as clean as possible. Once-fired glazes (ie those applied to the raw clayware before firing), normally dissolve some iron from the body and become discoloured. The degree of reaction between body and glaze is less if the clay body has already been fired before the glaze is applied.

2 Coloured glazes

These can be made from clear white glazes by adding colouring agents such as oxides or prepared stains. The addition of small amounts of oxides such as cobalt (blue), iron oxide (brown, yellow), chromium (green), nickel (khaki, brown, greenish colours), etc, produces clear coloured 'solution' glazes. The colouring oxides dissolve in the molten glaze, and sometimes the texture of the clay-body can be seen through the glaze. If prepared stains are used, the resulting coloured glaze is normally opaque and hides the underbody. The potter may prepare his own stains, or they can be purchased from colour suppliers. Examples of opacifying stains with good covering power are vanadium-zircon turquoise, chrome-tin pinks and selenium reds.

The way in which ceramic colours (including simple oxides) stain glazes is complex. For instance, when prepared stains are added to a clear glaze, some of the stain may be dissolved and later be precipitated on cooling to give desirable or undesirable effects. Stains may also alter the melting behaviour of glazes. For example, adding large amounts of copper oxide to lead glazes may cause the lead to become dangerously soluble so that the glazed pottery may constitute a health hazard to its users. Acids in foods may leach out the lead and cause poisoning.

Apart from the relatively simple method of colouring glazes mentioned above, it is possible to make coloured glazes by using frits that have the stain pre-melted in them. This is commonly done with zircon frits produced for opacified coloured glazes (see Section 1).

3 Opacified glazes

In the same way as clear water can be made turbid or cloudy by stirring up the mud from the bottom of a pond, it is possible to render a glaze opaque by suspending fine particles of solids in it. Sometimes minute gas bubbles may be present in a glaze, giving the effect of opacification. This milkiness may be a fault, or, as in the case of some artist glazes, it may add beauty to the glaze. When particles (either of solid or gas) are suspended in a glaze or enamel the light falling on the glaze is scattered and reflected from the surface. This makes the glass opaque.

Common opacifiers are zirconium dioxide, zircon and tin oxide. When tin oxide is simply added to a glaze, blended, and fired, the above simple mechanism of opacification may apply. The insoluble tin oxide particles reflect the light back into the eye of the viewer and the glaze appears opaque. However, the use of zircon is more complicated than that of tin. The zirconia (or zircon) is usually first dissolved by the glaze during firing, followed by precipitation during the cooling of the ware in the kiln. The particle sizes of the resulting crystals of opacifier have a critical bearing on the degree of opacity in the glaze.

Titanium dioxide is sometimes used as a frit opacifier for

metal enamels. The problem with titania, however, is the discolouration caused by the presence of even small traces of iron
oxide.

The proportions of opacifier required depend on the materials used, the composition of the glazes and the firing temperature. It is usual to make a series of tests, adding 1-10% of
opacifier to ten samples of glaze (ie 1-10% of material based
on the dry weight of the slop glaze). The samples should be
fired together to ensure strict comparability.

Tin oxide is usually added in amounts of 4-8% by weight.
Much more zircon or zirconia is needed (up to 15% in some
cases) to obtain a well opacified glaze or enamel. Since both
tin and zirconia are refractory materials, increasing the melting point of the glaze, their use is often accompanied by a need
for modifying the kiln temperatures. Sometimes it is necessary
to modify the base glaze by adding extra fluxes.

4 Crystalline glazes

Art and studio potters have a distinct advantage over the industrial potter in producing a wide range of crystalline glazes,
especially with regard to those glazes having coarse crystals,
protruding above the surface. The technique is suitable only
for small-scale production and, usually, the firing conditions
must be specially arranged for the glazing.

Briefly, crystalline glazes are made by saturating the glaze
with a colouring oxide and then allowing the glaze to cool
slowly in the kiln to give the crystals time to separate. The rate
of cooling determines the size of the crystals: the slower the
rate the bigger the crystals.

One of the earlier known forms of crystalline glazes was
coral red, made from chromates in high-lead fusions. The red
pigment was obtained by boiling chrome yellow (lead chromate) with dilute caustic soda solution until the bright red pigment developed as basic lead chromate [$PbCrO_4.Pb(OH)_2$].
This was then used to make crystalline red-orange glazes.
Their melting points were low and the firing cycle was difficult to control. With the development of selenium reds for
glazes maturing at about 950-1050°C, these coral reds have
gone out of use, mainly because of the hazard of lead poisoning
due to their high content of soluble lead. On vases and other

decorative ceramics not intended for food use, coral reds may be used to good effect by the art potter.

A starting formula for the development of coral red is:

$$\left. \begin{array}{ll} 0.752 & PbO \\ 0.065 & K_2O \\ 0.183 & Na_2O \end{array} \right\} \qquad \left\{ \begin{array}{ll} 0.060 & Al_2O_3 \\ 0.065 & Cr_2O_3 \end{array} \right. \qquad \left\{ \begin{array}{ll} 0.316 & SiO_2 \\ 0.100 & SnO_2 \end{array} \right.$$

The glaze matures at Seger cone 01 (1080°C). Slow cooling produces a distinctive, smooth crystalline effect. The selenium-cadmium glazes produced to replace coral reds mature at approximately the same temperatures as the old coral-red glazes.

Nickel oxide in most types of glaze is prone to crystallisation and can be used to obtain distinctive effects. According to J. W. Mellor, a certain way of obtaining crystals in a glaze is to use nickel oxide in the following fritted glaze (the bases do not add up to one in this formula):

$$\left. \begin{array}{ll} 0.063 & Na_2O \\ 0.086 & K_2O \\ 0.110 & CaO \\ 0.063 & BaO \\ 0.617 & ZnO \\ 0.013 & NiO \end{array} \right\} \qquad 0.038 \quad Al_2O_3 \qquad \left\{ \begin{array}{ll} 0.867 & SiO_2 \\ 0.038 & TiO_2 \\ 0.188 & B_2O_3 \end{array} \right.$$

The firing temperature is high, about 1280°, so the glaze might be suitable for stoneware. The full recipe and other information are given in Mellor's paper published in *Transactions English Ceramic Society* 13, 61, 1914.

5 Matte, vellum and satin glazes

These glazes are types of crystalline glazes but the crystals are so small as to be almost invisible to the naked eye. They are developed by selecting the appropriate chemical composition. Zinc mattes, for example, are due to zinc silicate crystallising on the surface. Lime matte glazes are due to calcium silicate (wollastonite) forming in the glaze.

Shiny glazes can be matted by adding materials such as talc, milled pitchers and calcined bone to the glaze. These materials may remain undissolved in the glaze and give the desired effect of matteness, though they are not properly crystalline mattes, for no crystallisation has occurred.

A relatively simple technique to obtain mattes is to dope a

low-temperature glaze with 12-18% of a mixture of equal parts of titania, tin oxide and zinc oxide. Sometimes the mixture is calcined before adding it to the glaze.

6 Vapour (salt) glazing

In the firing of many stoneware products such as drainpipes, jam jars and other storage vessels, if common salt is thrown into the fire at a certain point of the cycle, the products taken from the kiln will be found to be glazed with a bright clear film of glass. The use of salt glazing involves considerable difficulties for the art and craft potter because of the adverse effects of the salt on the kiln structure. Upon volatilisation, the salt vigorously attacks the refractories of the brickwork and may cause premature failure of the kiln structure.

Salt or vapour glazing may also be done with mixtures of salts, such as common salt and boric acid or borax. The process is carried out in the kiln at temperatures about 1110°C. The vapours formed when the salt is added to the fire coming into contact with the clay ware react with the aluminosilicates of the material, forming a glaze. The method is very old and, industrially at least, has almost universely been replaced by techniques involving the application of prepared glazes.

20 GLAZE-BODY ADHESION

Glazes are applied as milled powders suspended in water—glaze slips. The water is dried off and the resulting layer is heated in the glost kiln. The melting of the particles of glaze ingredients is followed by the formation of a glassy film. As the glass is formed and becomes fluid with the heat of the kiln there is some reaction with the underlying body. The surface of the clay is attacked and corroded by the melt which penetrates the underbody, forming an intermediate layer. The result of this glass formation, fusing, penetration and glass-body reaction is illustrated in Fig 15.

glaze surface

glaze slightly contaminated with body

clay body

Fig 15 Section through glazed pottery showing the gradual transition from the fired body, through the mixture of glass and fired clay, to the pure glass of the glaze film. The crystalline formations consist of various minerals such as wollastonite, mullite and other silicates

The nature and extent of this intermediate layer determines the properties of the glaze-body union and hence the strength, crazing resistance and other properties of the fired ware.

The type of glaze has a critical effect on the reaction between melt and underbody. Fluid glazes that melt at low temperatures such as high-lead and certain borate compositions will react more readily (forming a distinct intermediate layer) than say sluggish alkaline-silicate compositions, such as feldspathic glazes at any given temperature.

Glaze frit and crazing resistance

If a pottery glaze is to cover the clay body as a stable continuous film without cracking or flaking, owing to the stresses that may develop when the ware is heated and cooled (during firing and also in service), then the body and the skin must have accommodating or matching expansion factors. The intermediate layer which has a composition—and therefore an expansion behaviour—somewhat intermediate between glaze and body, will mitigate the effects of differences in expansion between glass and body. However, if the glass expands very much more than the body, the cooling film will contract more than the body (for it expanded more in firing or heating) and it usually tears, cracks appearing in the glaze film. The network of cracks on glazed pottery is called *crazing*.

Some idea of the magnitude of the difference in the expansion of glaze and body may be obtained from the size of the mesh of crazing: the finer the network the greater the difference. It is also important to note that the expansion of the glaze should not equal precisely that of the underbody, for the entire glazed article is much stronger when the glass film grips the clay body, that is, when the glaze is under *compression*.

21 CONTROLLING CRAZING AND PEELING

Advice is often given to 'add some flint to the body', or 'put some talc in the mix', or 'fire harder', or 'reduce the thickness of the glaze coating'. Sometimes these measures may work. However, altering the composition of the body or glaze or changing the firing cycle without knowing for certain the cause of the crazing epidemic in potteries is usually asking for trouble from other faults.

Soon, the use of these 'hit or miss' methods disturbs the balance of the body and glaze composition and the firing cycle so much that the only logical step is to return to the position that existed when crazing broke out. It is axiomatic that before any additions or alterations are made to the production cycle—the term is applicable to artist's output as well as large scale activities—a series of simple trials should be made to determine the effects of the alterations.

The factor that affects crazing and peeling has been stated to be the relative expansions of glaze and body. But which factors govern that effect? They are 1. The chemical composition of body and glaze. 2. The texture of the clayware, that is, its porosity and the nature of the pores—whether they are mainly dead-end pores (sealed) or communicating (unsealed). 3. The content and types of silica present, that is, free quartz, cristobalite, and tridymite.

Information will be found relating to the effects of 1. in the sections of this book covering compositions and physical properties. The texture of the body is important because a porous body absorbs moisture from the air as soon as it leaves the kiln. This moisture causes the body to expand and if the glaze skin is not compressing hard enough, the body's expansion overcomes the compression, and the glaze crazes. Briefly, this is

why vitrified, glassy bodies such as porcelains and well-formu-
lated stoneware do not craze as easily as earthenware and
majolica.

The question may be asked: how does the moisture enter
the body if it is coated with glaze? Usually the back of the ware
or the feet of cups, for example, contain small unglazed spots
or patches where they have been supported in the kiln.

Under 3. we come to the effects of silica crystal inversions
or transformations.

Effects of silica changes on crazing

The first point to note is that it is the silica in the body that
is under discussion and particularly the free or *uncombined*
silica. The silica in the glaze is usually of secondary importance in considering crazing. The silica in pottery bodies may
also be present in the chemically combined state, ie, as silicates
or as aluminosilicates. For example, clays are mixtures of
aluminosilicates and in them the silica is mainly in the combined form. On the other hand, sand is almost pure silica in
the quartz form and the whole of the sand or quartz present in
a raw body is considered to be in the free state until the
materials are fired.

As soon as heat is applied in the kiln, of course, some of the
free silica (added as sand or potter's flint) may combine chemically with other ingredients such as the whiting or alkalis to
form silicates. When this happens the amount of free silica is
reduced. The properties of the fired body will depend on the
amount of free silica left after firing is complete.

In the preparation of commercial earthenware bodies free
silica is added as one of the main ingredients. Sand (quartz) or
flint (cryptocrystalline quartz) may be added to the ball clays,
the kaolin and the feldspar to make up the body. A chemical
analysis will show that such a body contains about 75% silica
but only about 40% is left in the free state after firing. It is
this free silica that makes pottery resist crazing. In unpurified
clays the free silica content may vary very widely.

*How does the behaviour of free silica in the body affect the
crazing resistance of the glaze?* As discussed above, crazing is
affected by the expansions of body and glaze. During the heating of the body containing free silica (quartz or any of its other

forms), volume changes occur that are not due to the simple reversible expansion and contraction of a body undergoing heating and cooling, such as when an iron bar expands and contracts. These volume changes are due to the presence of the quartz. And the size of the changes depends on the form of the silica crystals.

When, during heating and cooling, the atoms of silicon and oxygen that make up the crystal of silica rearrange themselves, the space they occupy alters. These spatial alterations are called *crystal inversions* or transformations (Fig 16). It is the

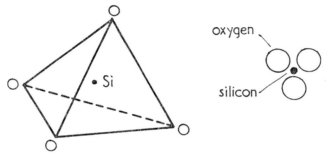

Fig 16 Four oxygen atoms surround one silicon atom to form a silica tetrahedron—the building block of many silicates, sand, flint and other ceramic materials. The positions in space taken up by the atoms during heating and cooling alter, a process called crystal inversion

inversions that decide how the body behaves in relation to the glaze. For example, one spatial arrangement of the silicon and oxygen atoms (SiO_2) is called cristobalite. The others are quartz and tridymite. Now if the body being fired contains much cristobalite, the danger of cracking (dunting) is high, since at about 225°C cristobalite expands by 3% of its volume during firing. If this expansion takes place rapidly there is a distinct danger of the ware cracking.

However, the potter tries to develop a small amount of cristobalite in his fired body because when it has cooled the *shrinkage* taking place at the same temperature (225°C) puts the glaze under compression relative to the body and, as we noted above, this is one of the conditions for a highly crazing resistant glaze. The ways in which silica alters its forms during heating and cooling and the significance of this behaviour are discussed more fully in Section 4.

The crazing behaviour of glasses is affected by the form of the silica, its grain-size distribution and the amount in the body. If flint is used, the normal practice is to calcine it with a small amount (2%) of lime to make it easier to grind and to produce a small amount of cristobalite. The difference between the behaviour of the two main forms of silica (quartz sand and flint) used in potteries is important. Calcined potter's flint pebbles are easier to grind, show a less abrupt alpha-beta quartz inversion (see Section 4), and therefore are less prone to dunting and cracking, and also cause easier vitrification of the body.

Potter's flint used in Britain and in some American potteries is a cryptocrystalline form of silica, that is, it is made up of very fine (*crypto* = hidden) crystals compared with the coarse crystals of quartz sand.

Peeling of glazes

This is sometimes described as the opposite fault to crazing. In fact, it is a fault that develops by putting the glaze *excessively* under compression. Peeling occurs when the expansions of glaze and body are at variance. The remedy is to reduce the contraction of the body or increase that of the glaze. Peeling is not as common as crazing because body and glaze will stand up to compression much better than tension.

Fig 17 shows the relative movement of glaze-body systems under different conditions. When the glaze is molten it covers the body (L-L); when the article is cooled the glaze tries to contract to position x-x but cannot do so because it is stuck to the body. In other words, the glaze skin is holding the glaze under compression (like a fist clenching a marble). The result is a high crazing resistance because the compressive strength of the glaze is high. Note that it is the relative shrinkage of the body and the glaze that have caused this net result.

In Fig 17b peeling would result since the glaze has contracted less than the body which is therefore in tension. Since the tensile strength of the glazes is not high, the net effect is a break in the glaze (peeling). Under the conditions illustrated in Fig 17b the net effect may be to cause bowing or distortion.

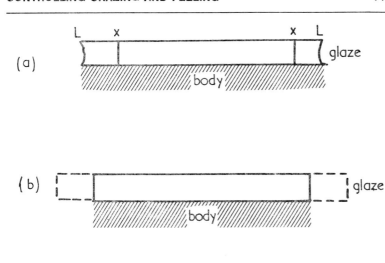

Fig 17   Behaviour of glaze skin on body during firing and cooling illustrating the mechanism of crazing (see text for explanations)

As the body contracts, it pulls the skin of glaze around into a peel to conform to its own movement towards sphericity. Yet another effect is that the glazed ware may shatter (dunting).

From the above, it will be clear just how important are the relative expansions of glaze and body. The chemical composition of the glaze and body, the form of the silica, and the firing temperatures must all be controlled to give a properly balanced relationship.

22 APPLYING GLAZES TO POTTERY

Glazes are used as slips, that is, suspensions of solids in water. Small amounts of plastic clay or bentonite may be used to keep the heavier particles of frit and other solids in suspension.

In glazing pottery that has been fired once (biscuit state) a possible difficulty is that the glaze slip needs to be altered to match the porosity of the biscuit. Highly porous ware will suck up more glaze (water) when dipped in it than vitrified ware and so a consistently thick glaze layer can only be obtained by changing the density (pint weight) or the viscosity of the glaze slip.

Thickening of glazes

Glazes may be thickened by adding certain chemical compounds such as calcium chloride. A fairly safe practical procedure is to use a saturated solution of calcium chloride (made by adding calcium chloride to water until more of it fails to dissolve). In the pottery this solution is then used in very small amounts (spoonfuls per gallon of glaze) to adjust the thickness (viscosity) and suit the ware being glazed.

Other chemical dopes suitable for this purpose include ammonium chloride, acetic acid (vinegar) and borax (for enamels).

Since dipping is a skilled process, the potter will usually know from experience the desired consistency of his glaze and will use the dope to produce the required effects. Adding chemical dopes to slip glazes does not alter the density (pint weight) of the glaze; it merely alters the consistency by coagulating (flocculating) the particles in the slip. The process is the opposite of deflocculation described in Section 2 (Casting Slips).

Drying of the glaze

After the glaze has been applied to the ware, it is a simple process to dry it but care should be taken not to disturb the tender film of glaze. In this state it consists of particles held together by the green bond—usually the clay. If the glaze films are so weak that handling causes them to break up or flake off the ware, a possible answer is to use a hardening agent such as gum or cellulose derivative (e.g. carboxy-methyl cellulose). These chemicals toughen the dried glaze before firing and eliminate mechanical damage in handling. The use of carboxy-methyl cellulose requires special care, especially in dispersing it in the glaze. Manufacturer's instructions should be followed.

In most small potteries, glazed ware ready for firing is dried by placing it on shelves or tables and letting the warmth of the workshop remove the moisture. Some of the water in the glaze is absorbed into the body and, in the initial firing period, must be allowed to leave the ware slowly, to avoid pressure that would force the glaze off the ware, or cause other damage.

The industrial application of glazes involves the use of mechanised methods such as spray guns, cascade dipping, conveyors, and so on. Naturally where the potter's skill cannot be depended on, as in mechanical dipping, the consistency of the glaze slips must be controlled within correspondingly closer limits of tolerance.

The thickness of glazes

This of course, determines their fired appearance. Stoneware, for instance, depends critically on the marriage between glaze and clay. The thickness of the fired glaze film may be important in earthenware and similar bodies especially for lead (transparent or coloured) glazes fired at moderate temperatures. The higher the firing temperature used, the less critical is the relationship between glaze and body in terms of crazing resistance and strength. It seems that the fire evens out the stresses.

23   TYPES OF METAL ENAMELS

As in glazes, the various types of enamels, frits and glasses used for metal decoration and protection in the craft of metal enamelling can be classified in several ways. For instance, they can be classified by physical appearance or by chemical composition. Under physical appearance, there are opaque, transparent and opalescent types. The classification by chemical composition depends on the type of metal for which the enamel is being developed, the firing temperature, and frequently whether the materials are to be applied to vessels employed for food use.

A third approach in classifying enamels is that of purpose. For example, the enamels used for steel will be quite different from those developed for copper and aluminium. Copper enamels are usually simple lead silicates with additions of alkalis and sometimes opacifiers such as tin oxide and titania. Aluminium enamels may contain lead, phosphates and barium and others.

From the descriptions in this book of glass-forming materials and reactions it will be clear that all enamels are basically glasses or frits. The glasses may be formed either prior to application or *in situ* on the metal. The commonest technique is to prepare fusible frits, crush and grind them, and then by various techniques such as sprinkling, spraying or dipping, to apply these powders to the metal, followed by firing.

Table 18 shows the component range of the various oxides used in most enamels.

The materials shown in Table 18 are used for making clear enamels. The colouring and opacifying effects are obtained by adding other materials such as colouring oxides, prepared pigments, and much higher contents of zirconia, zircon, and some-

TABLE 18
OXIDE RANGE FOR METAL ENAMEL COMPOSITIONS

Oxide	% by weight	Oxide	% by weight
		TiO_2	0-10
B_2O_3	0-20	PbO	0-60
Na_2O (K_2O)	12-30	ZnO	0-15
F	0-15	BaO	0-15
Al_2O_3	0-12	MgO	0-3
CaO	0-10	ZrO_2	0-10

times tin oxide. Titanium dioxide is also a common opacifier in metal enamels.

Basic approach to composition

As in other glasses, silica is the main component of enamels. Since its fusion point is too high for the formation of glass films on metals, the silica must be modified to reduce this fusion point. We therefore add alkalis such as soda and potassia to reduce the melting point. The simple glasses thus obtained, of course, are not very stable chemically and other agents must be added to increase the stability. Boric oxide which also reduces the expansion factor is commonly used as an enamel flux.

Certain fluorides may be added with the same purpose in mind. The methods in which the basic fluxed silicates are stabilised to give useful enamel frits have been described in Section 2.

Thermal expansion

This is a very important factor in compiling any enamel frit for metals. The coefficient of thermal expansion of enamels varies widely; the greater the metal thickness, then the more closely should the expansion of enamel match that of the metal. The exact differences between the coefficients for metal and enamel will depend on the particular combinations. For example, a difference of only 10% for enamelled iron may produce cracking or scaling, whereas the difference for enamelled silver may safely be more than 100%.

In general, the expansion of enamels should be less than that of the metal being coated in order to put the glass coat under compression (see under Glazes). The expansion factors

of enamels needs to be different for the different types of shapes
being coated. To guarantee thermal and mechanical strength
in the coatings the expansion factors of enamel and metal for
convex surfaces should be as close as possible. On the other
hand, for concave surfaces a distinct difference in the factors is
permitted, especially when the coating needs to have a high
thermal-shock resistance, such as when it is to be used in boiling water followed by sudden cooling.

Steel enamels

Before the final coat of enamel can be applied to ordinary
steels it is sometimes necessary to apply a ground enamel and
this of course complicates the technique considerably. However, special enamels (titania based) are now in use not requir-
ing grounds. If silver-plated steel is used, the need for the
ground coat is eliminated, and the procedure is identical to
that for coating ordinary silver with enamel.

A ground enamel is the intermediate layer between the
metal and the cover enamel. It creates a strong bond between
the various metals and the glass. The main feature of the
ground enamel is its content of bonding oxides, such as about
1% cobalt oxide and other oxides such as nickel. The amount
of cobalt or nickel oxide varies, and for sheet steel thicknesses
of 0·5-1mm, about 0·5% cobalt oxide is suitable.

The concentration of nickel oxide in ground enamels for
steel is usually about 1·5-2%. The oxides of nickel and cobalt,
of course, are strong colourants. When the cover coat enamel is
applied, the undercoat colour may show through. Suppliers
now offer white grounds containing zirconia, antimony and
cerium oxides which do not have these faults. Suppliers of
sheet steel for enamelling can usually recommend suitable
enamelling compositions for grounds and cover coats. A rough
guide to the composition of grounds for steel is: 17-21% B_2O_3,
50-55% SiO_2, and 15-22% alkalis. The content of cobalt, nickel
and manganese oxides is around 3% for good bonding. The
other 10% is usually made up of calcium oxide (4-6%) and
alumina (3-7%). Various other materials (see Table 19) are
also used.

Page 149 Separately moulded pieces of clay are attached to a green vase before firing. The chemical composition of decorative pieces and the vase is such that in firing they bond together. The clay must be in the ideal condition for 'sticking up' in this skilled operation (*courtesy Wedgwood & Sons Ltd*)

Page 150 *(above)* Complicated figures are made by casting the parts separately and then sticking them together. Here plaster moulds are being opened *(courtesy Rosenthal-Porzellan)*;

(right) ceramics are fired by placing them on refractory kiln furniture such as these Gimson open setters. Various structures can be built up on the kiln car for placing various kinds of ware. The materials are made of high-grade refractory compositions such as sillimanite, alumina, special fireclays, and silicon carbide, depending on firing conditions;

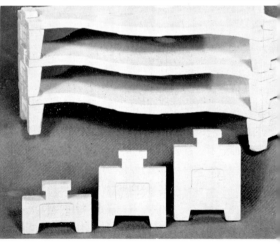

(bottom right) the Gimson 'Paragon' crank system for supporting ware for firing. These kiln furniture structures can be built up rapidly and effectively to protect the ware and reduce loss due to sticking of ware and furniture *(courtesy J. Gimson)*

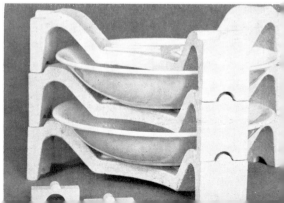

Cover enamels

Cover enamels are made decorative by staining or opacifying them so that when they are applied on top of the ground enamel they enhance and of course protect the metal base. The main properties are brilliance, glossiness, evenness of colour and any individual effects developed by the enameller.

White enamels

These are usually based on titanium, antimony and various fluorides. The opacifiers can be added to the batch, before the frits are made, or to the mill for grinding.

If the opacifiers are added to the mill, it is found that the composition of the enamel has little effect on the strength of the opacification. However, if the opacifiers are incorporated with the frit during the melting of the enamel glasses, then the chemical composition of the base glass will have a critical effect on the opacification strength. In other words, sometimes no matter how much opacifying agent is added to the frit, if the chemical composition is not suitable, no opacifying effect will result.

Opacified white enamels

Enamels containing fluorine are based on the use of fluorides and normally contain up to 12% fluorine. The opacification is due to the separation of crystals of sodium fluoride and to some extent calcium fluoride. Very small amounts of fluorine (below 3%) will increase the fluidity of the frits, sometimes without producing opacification. As the fluorine content rises, fluorides crystallise from the melt and this produces opacification. The chemistry of fluorine enamels is rather complicated and, although these are also used to produce a wide range of coloured enamels in industry, the art potter needs special care in using them. Instructions provided with commercial fluorine enamels should be followed very carefully.

White enamels based on antimony

In this case the opacification results from the crystallisation of antimoniates. The important point about these is that antimony is toxic and therefore cannot be used in enamels designed for vessels that are to be used in cooking or for serving food.

κ

Zircon enamels

Since zircon is non-toxic and a very stable compound, its use in metal enamels would be very extensive if it were not for the great increase in the refractoriness of the frit when zircon is added. Furthermore, most common frits will dissolve up to 15% of zirconium dioxide without inducing opacification. Another disadvantage with zircon opacified enamels is that because of their low silica content they are not very acid resistant. They soon lose their shininess.

Phosphate enamels

These owe their opacification to the crystallisation of calcium phosphate, taking place during the fritting, an effect which is enhanced when the enamel is fired (or repeatedly fired). The phosphate enamel range is responsible for matte enamels, but the coatings are often brittle. Double application of enamel is often commonplace where this material is used but currently the phosphate enamel composition is becoming out of date.

White enamels based on *titanium* owe their opacification to titanium dioxide crystallising either as anatase or rutile when the enamel is fired. Opacification depends on the refractive index of titania and the values for rutile and anatase are very high.

The other advantages of titania enamels include high acid resistance and great whiteness. Single applications will often produce very intense degrees of opacification and coverage. The enamels also have high thermal-shock resistance and impact and bending strengths. White titanium enamels are probably the most popular of all white opacified enamels because of their absolute safety in use and the above valuable technical properties.

A serious fault with titanium enamels is their proneness to yellowing. This is dependent on many factors, including the crystal form and size of the opacifying crystals, the presence of iron oxide and chromium oxide and reduction conditions in firing.

Coloured metal enamels

Colour effects are obtained simply by adding colouring ox-

TABLE 19

CHEMICAL COMPOSITION OF SOME WHITE ENAMELS

Components	Titania			Fluoride	Zircon
	(1)	(2)	(3)		
SiO_2	41·5	38·6	48·8	59·5	35·6
TiO_2	16·4	17·3	17·3	—	—
P_2O_5	2·1	2·4	3·9	—	2·4
B_2O_3	16·2	19·8	7·7	7·9	14·6
Al_2O_3	6·1	4·5	4·1	11·7	9·5
MgO	1·7	1·5	2·6	—	—
K_2O	—	} 15·9	—	20·9	14·2
Na_2O	16·0		—		3·2
ZrO_2	—	—	—	—	15·0
CaO	—	—	—	—	5·5
TOTAL	100·0	100·0	100·0	100·0	100·0
+Fluorine	6·2	2·5	6·5	8·6	13·4

ides to the batch when preparing the frits or adding specially prepared pigments, obtainable from ceramic colour suppliers, during the grinding of the frit. As in the formulation of coloured glazes, the use of the numerous colourants available in various amounts by the art enameller may yield a wide range of colours, both standard and individual. Experimentation with raw colouring oxides as well as prepared stains will produce the desired effects.

Colourants in the form of oxides are added to the raw materials used to produce transparent enamels only when dark enamels are being obtained, for instance, blue containing 2% cobalt oxide, or violet containing up to 10% manganese dioxide. Blacks are made by adding a carefully balanced combination of various oxides.

It is possible to stain opacified enamels by making various additions of colourant such as cobalt, cobalt and copper, copper and chromium, and so on. The chemical composition of the frit will obviously affect the final colours. For example, highly opacified enamels often become greyish when black stains are added. Brilliant coloured enamels can be produced by using faintly opacified bases such as those obtained with fluorides. Pastel coloured shades can be obtained with titania opacified enamels. Very pleasing pastel shades in metal enamels are obtained with yellow pigments such as those obtained from 0·2% chromium oxide or 2% nickel and also violet, obtained by adding 1·5-2% manganese dioxide.

Luminescent enamels

Luminescence is obtained by adding special chemicals, such as zinc sulphite, which have been activated by the chemical supplier with traces of copper and other heavy metals. Specially prepared agents, known as luminophors, are added to the enamel slip in amounts of up to 30%. The base enamel or frit should be fusible and should be moderate in acid components such as silica and boric acid. A typical composition for a luminescent enamel is given as 24·8% SiO_2, 25·8 TiO_2, 10·9 B_2O_3, 1·0 Sb_2O_3, 5·0 ZnO, 6·9 K_2O, 18·9 Na_2O, 4·0 Li_2O, and 2·7 parts by weight of fluorine on 100 parts of enamel. In enamel production on an industrial scale, luminescent enamels are used for technical purposes and will light up in the dark for only short periods. Permanently luminescing enamels are made by incorporating radioactive isotopes.

Enamels for aluminium and other metals

As mentioned above, the composition of an enamel must be formulated specifically for the type of metal to which it is to be applied. Normally the supplier of the powders to art and craft enamellers will specify a range of different compositions to suit different metals.

Aluminium enamels should be very fusible and have a high thermal expansion to suit the melting point of pure aluminium (659°C). The thermal expansion coefficient of aluminium is almost double that of iron.

Suitable compositions for aluminium can be produced by using frits with high concentrations of alkalis and low silica concentrations. It is normal practice to add large amounts of lead oxide and titania. Together with the low silica content, this causes aluminium enamels to have poor chemical resistance and they therefore do not satisfy the requirements placed on enamels used in cooking vessels. In recent years new types of highly resistant aluminium enamels have been developed. These, covered by patents, contain high proportions of lead and various amounts of boric oxide. In addition leadless enamels have been produced for application to aluminium and have a high resistance to acids, and stable colouring properties.

During the bonding of enamel and metal in aluminium structures (see below), the bond is achieved through the film of alumina (aluminium oxide) which develops when freshly processed aluminium metal is exposed to the atmosphere. Some types of aluminium enamels can be fired at temperatures of 520-580° in specially designed furnaces to give very thin glass films so that the enamel sheet can be drilled and sheared without adversely affecting the coating. With the development of aluminium structures in architecture, as mentioned in Section 1, the manufacturer of glass enamels for metals has concentrated on the production of weather resistant enamels and current developments indicate that the enamelling of aluminium will represent a major development in the craft. This is a strong challenge to art and craft enamellers wishing to use the medium not only for producing small artefacts such as vases, plaques, etc, but also for large scale constructions such as the frontages of buildings, etc.

Non-ferrous and noble metal enamels

The enamel compositions developed for gold, silver, copper and their alloys are very diverse and must match the varying thermal expansion factors of these metals. The basic composition for such enamels is usually high in lead, and the main constituent is a lead-potassium silicate. Antimony is also used for opacifying many decorative enamels for noble metals and for copper.

Table 20 shows enamels for aluminium and copper.

TABLE 20
ENAMELS FOR ALUMINIUM AND COPPER

Oxides	Aluminium		Copper (also for gold and silver)		Red (Ruby)
	Lead	Leadless	Clear, Coloured	Opaque	
SiO_2	29·2	36·6	39·4	31·4	38·1
TiO_2	11·5	24·7	—	—	—
B_2O_3	5·5	4·0	0·4	1·7	1·7
PbO	24·9	—	43·2	54·4	42·5
K_2O	10·4	—	15·6	6·5	14·8
Na_2O	11·7	30·7	0·2	0·8	0·7
Li_2O	2·8	4·0	—	—	—
SnO_2	—	—	—	—	0·5
Sb_2O_3	4·0	—	—	—	0·5
As_2O_3	—	—	1·2	5·2	1·2
Au	—	—	—	—	0·03-0·07

*Coloured enamels are made by adding 0·1-3·0% CoO, Cr_2O_3, CuO, etc.

24 ENAMEL-METAL BOND

When the powdered enamel has been applied to the metal underbody and fired, providing certain technical requirements have been met, the heat of the furnace fuses the enamel frit and bonds it to the metal. The precise manner in which the frit is bonded to the metal is the subject of research. Several theories exist about it.

Obviously the fluid enamel in the furnace must coat or wet the metal. The surface of the metal must be clean and free from grease and other agents that would prevent the molten glass running smoothly over the metal and wetting it. However, for some metals, absolutely clean non-oxidised surfaces will not be wetted by the melting enamel and it is necessary, as for example with iron and steel, to apply a ground coat. The enamel fusion will also hold onto the rough surface better than the smooth.

As mentioned above in the section on Enamel Composition, certain special additives are made to ground enamels to improve bonding. These include cobalt, nickel, antimony, arsenic, molybdenum and other oxides. The bond between frit and gold, silver and platinum, for example, is due mainly to purely mechanical effects: there is very little chemical corrosion or reaction between glass and metal. What happens is that a very thin film of oxide develops on the surface of the metal during the initial heating process and this oxide is wetted and partly absorbed by the enamel melt, providing a holding layer for the enamel. It is common practice therefore when enamelling metals such as gold, silver and platinum to roughen the surfaces. The melting enamel then flows into the cavities and holds on to the surface.

When copper is being enamelled, the bonding occurs on

smooth surfaces. This is due to the layer of cuprous oxide formed on the metal. This layer of oxide can be noted even with the naked eye. The oxide is usually dissolved in the enamel and helps to form a strong bond.

When iron is being enamelled, it is particularly important to roughen the surface and on an industrial scale this is done by sand blasting.

The most complicated bonding mechanism is that which occurs when metal enamels are applied to steel. The theories about the precise nature of the bond are very complicated and so far specialists have no single opinion. Various ideas about the formation of intermediate oxide layers (compare the formation of intermediate layers in ceramics), electro-chemical processes and other mechanisms have been discussed in technical works.

In Section 2 an account was given of the preparation of metals following shaping, prior to the application of the enamel. This preparation consists of cleaning and pickling the metal articles so as to present a clean and receptive surface to the fusing enamel when it is subjected to firing. The process of pickling consists in immersing the metals in aqueous solutions of mineral acids such as hydrochloric, sulphuric, acetic, and sometimes phosphoric acids.

Pickling involves a reaction between acids and oxides of iron (scale) to form soluble salts and also the mechanical rubbing of the scale from the surface of the metal. Naturally the degree of pickling or chemical reaction between the acids and metals will increase when more highly concentrated acids are used. The maximum reaction for hydrochloric acids occurs at a concentration of 20%, and for sulphuric it is about 25%. Above this there is scarcely any increase in the reaction. For art and craft enamelling much lower concentrations (about 6%) are normally employed, especially for such metals as copper and iron.

The effect of increasing the temperature of the pickling solution is to increase the rate of the pickling process and, in the industry, acid temperatures of up to 90°C are used, although in a workshop such as the art-enamel studio this is impracticable. Great care should be used with the handling of acids of any concentrations or temperature. When the metals react with the acids, hydrogen is given off according to the well known reaction between acids and metals and this hydrogen gas may accumulate in the metal. Frequently when the enamelled metal is fired, the hydrogen will produce certain faults such as bubbling and fish-scaling (small semicircles of enamel flake off). The hydrogen absorption depends on the metal structure, the state of its surface, the thickness of the article being processed, the impurity content, the solution temperature, the pickling time, and other factors.

The pickling of silver prior to enamelling is often done in nitric acid solutions so as to enrich the surface with silver and improve the microgeometrical surface of the metal. The bonding between enamel and silver is dependent on developing a suitable micro-relief surface.

Copper and its alloys prior to enamelling are sometimes pickled in a mixture of one part by weight of sulphuric acid, one part of concentrated nitric acid, and 0·1 parts of common salt. The articles are then immersed in this solution, washed and dried.

25 APPLYING METAL ENAMELS

By powdering

A powdered enamel, which may be bought as powder, or as slabs of frit and crushed and ground by the operator, is applied by sprinkling or powdering it directly onto the metal. So that it will stick in a uniform coat on the metal, the latter is first coated with a thin and uniform film of adhesive such as tragancanth glue or other suitable material. The powdered enamel may be applied through a coarse screen (a tea strainer will serve) to aid in its distribution over the article. The coat of powder is then gently dried and is then ready for firing. Its thickness should be about the same as that of the metal to which it is applied.

Slip or wet method

The wet technique may involve dipping, pouring or spraying. The milled enamel frit in the form of a slip is stirred before the metal articles are dipped. A certain degree of skill is required to obtain a uniform and thin coating. The usual thickness is 0·1-0·15mm. The coating power of enamel slips is governed by the chemical nature of the slip, the degree of grinding and ageing of the material, the presence of doping agents and temperature. It is usual to age enamel slips to make them more stable before use. Excessively cold slips are prone to segregation and irregular application. Moist enamel powder is used with palette knives for application to small items such as jewellery.

The *grinding* of frits and enamels in water for application to metal is a critical process. If enamels are bought from suppliers in the form of powders they will need to be blended with water and screened in order to produce a creamy, smooth slip of the required bulk density.

However, if the art enameller prepares his own frits by fusion, or purchases his enamels in slab or granular form they will have to be milled, usually in small ball mills or edge-runner mills. Hand grinding, using a mortar and pestal, save for very small amounts or for samples, is a laborious job and variable results may be obtained if the job of grinding has to be repeated. This is not to say that the artist enameller working on individual creations should not manually grind his enamels.

Storage of enamel slips

Galvanised steel containers or rubber-lined vessels are suitable for storing enamel slips. They should be covered at all times to avoid contamination. After a certain time slips left to stand will start to settle out, leaving a layer of clear water on the top. If a thicker or heavier slip is required this clear water can be removed. To prevent compaction and setting on the bottom of containers the slip should be stirred periodically, using wooden paddles if mechanical stirrers are not available. Frequent screening will have the same desirable effect of keeping the slip uniform. Enamelled metal containers should not be used for storing slips since the electrochemical action of the container on the suspension causes rapid settling and setting in the bottom.

Doping enamel slips (See under Glazes)

Since metals are not porous, the viscosity of the enamel slip need not be altered to take account of porosity variations in the articles being dipped or sprayed. However, the metal enameller can often profitably use the doping principle in handling articles of different size and shape, to prevent running or curtaining for example.

Applying enamel slips to metals calls for skill. Enamel slips should have that consistency from which it is possible to produce a thin, uniform layer that holds on to the metal without running, or causing other faults. Slip that needs a great deal of shaking in the dipping process is usually too thick and would benefit by doping to reduce its viscosity.

Borax and soda-ash dopes are used for enamel frits. The

artist can prepare a small quantity, say a pint or litre, of a saturated solution of borax or soda ash and store this in a glass bottle for regular use. Only very small amounts should be added to the dipping vessel, otherwise the slip will be dispersed and not thickened. Over-doped slips should be corrected by adding untreated slip, not water or other chemicals.

26 COVERING CAPACITY OF ENAMELS

The way in which an enamel slip runs over and coats the metal depends on its density, viscosity and grain-size distribution. The stability of the slip, its settling rate, is also relevant. Any segregation of, say, lead frit or other heavy particles will produce patchy enamels after firing.

A simple test to determine the covering capacity is to weigh and immerse a small clean steel cylinder in the enamel, withdraw it slowly, allow the excess to run off and reweigh it. The weight of the amount of slip that has adhered to the cylinder gives a guide to how the slip will behave when used to coat the metal ware.

27 SPRAYING ENAMELS

Simple spraying techniques, using manually operated guns or air brushes, are now commonly used in metal enamelling. The advantages include greater uniformity of coating, higher application rates and ease of working, especially with large articles. Some very large articles such as plaques and architectural components can only be enamelled by spraying since they are too cumbersome to be dipped into slip.

Engineering suppliers usually issue instructions with air guns and spraying devices for dismantling and cleaning them. If organic solvents and media are used, as for example in applying metallic lustres, the mechanism of the gun may quickly become clogged up and rendered unworkable.

The viscosity, density and other rheological properties of enamel slips used for spraying must be controlled to give consistent results.

In order to improve the spraying technique and accelerate drying, it is usual to add de-natured alcohol to the water-enamel slip in preparing it. The ratio of water to alcohol may be 3 : 1. With more alcohol, the drying rate is accelerated.

The use of *organic media* such as resins and lacquers, dissolved or dispersed in various solvents, is also common practice among experienced art enamellers. Suppliers can produce enamel-media preparations ready for use, or the enameller may obtain the media separately and blend them to suit his requirements.

Turpentine and fat oil have long been excellent painting media in the ceramics industry and among art potters. This combination is also suitable for mixing enamels for painting as well as for blending highly viscous slips for the high-pressure spraying of large items, in which the usual water-enamel blends would present difficulties with running and other faults of application.

section 4

THE FIRING PROCESS

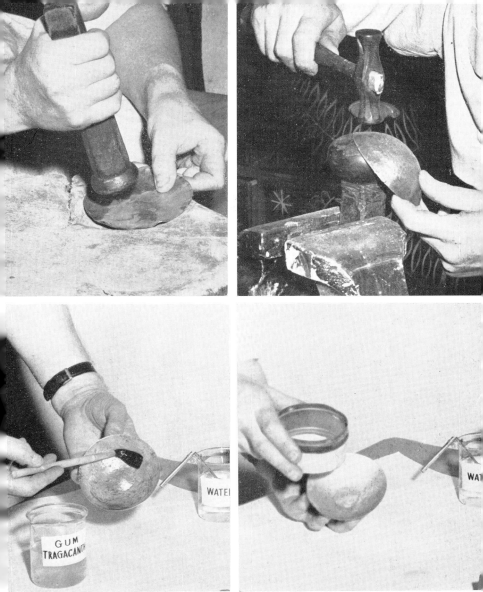

Page 167 *(top left)* The simple metal enamelling process begins by hammering out a disc of copper or other metal on a hard wood log. The disc is pounded with the steel stake and revolved to produce a bowl shape. A cavity is cut in the log to facilitate this operation; *(top right)* the bowl shape is then planished on a round-head steel stake placed in a vice. Attractive surface effects are obtained with the hammer which show through clear enamels after firing. The piece is then cleaned and scoured with steel wool. scouring powder and water; *(below left)* powdered enamel will not stick to dry uncoated metal, so the piece is coated with a thin film of gum and water; *(below right)* enamel powder ground to 80 mesh is screened on to the bowl freshly coated with adhesive. A light spray of water using a mouth blower is used to dampen the enamel powder *(courtesy Edward Winter)*

Page 168 (above) Edward Winter, pioneer enameller in the USA, is seen here firing the bowl resting inverted on chromel tripods wired to the chromel screen; (below) clay articles that are to be turned after rough shaping by other methods must be in the leather or cheese-hard state. Great precision is used to shave off the surplus clay to the desired outline and size. The motion of the lathe is then reversed and the turner burnishes the inside of the ware with a smooth steel tool (courtesy Wedgwood & Sons Ltd)

THE FIRING PROCESS

The work of the potter and enameller is completed by heat. All stages in shaping, drying and embellishing the ware ultimately must be tried by fire. The heat of the kiln or furnace converts clays into pottery (ceramic) and ground frits into enamels. The factors in any firing process are 1. The maximum temperatures used. 2. The rate of heating (how fast the temperatures are allowed to rise). 3. The time taken to reach the temperatures, and how long they are maintained. 4. The rate of cooling. All these factors are important in firing pottery and enamels, though some are more critical than others. For example, metal enamels can be fired and cooled much more quickly than glazed pottery (in periods of seconds or minutes, compared with hours or days).

Heat work

Simply, ceramic reactions depend on temperature and time. The potter, for instance, uses the term 'soak' to describe the time for which an article in the kiln is heated. The word arises from the concept that the pottery is being soaked in heat as if heat were a fluid that had to permeate the pores of the pottery and convert it from clay to 'burnt stuff' (one meaning of the word *keramos,* the Greek word for ceramics).

Thus, the term 'heat-work' becomes useful, because it takes into account not only the temperature but also the time of the process. Above certain critical temperatures, leaving the ware to soak longer is equivalent to raising the temperature. However, the idea of heat work being a simple product of temperature and time, if taken to extremes, turns out to be absurd: a piece of clayware would never change to pottery at temperatures below 200°C even if soaked for a million years!

L

Firing reactions

When clays and potter's materials are fired and when frits are fused on to enamels, the reactions include: thermal expansion, decomposition of compounds, oxidation, reduction, solid solution; crystal changes, sintering and vitrification (see below).

Purpose of firing

Clayware is fired because it is the only method of changing the soft, brittle, slakeable clay into hard, strong unslakeable ceramic. The function of the fire is to make permanently hard, durable materials from those that can be easily fragmented. Glass skins are applied to metals and pottery in order to protect them and to enhance their appearance.

Texture of ceramics

The nature of the raw materials and the way in which they are heated determines the texture of the finished article. Textures range from light, porous, soft-fired bodies, such as some insulating bricks or certain majolica bodies, to hard glassy materials with fine smooth surfaces, such as glasses, glazes and metal enamels. The practical implications of such textural differences are that unprotected, porous articles absorb moisture and cannot therefore be used in wet environments, whereas glassy materials are impervious to moisture. Furthermore, porous materials do not conduct heat so well as dense and so light pore-filled ceramics (insulating bricks, for instance) can be used to keep the heat inside kilns and furnaces.

Dimensional changes

Taking place when pottery and metals are being fired these may cause distortion or even cracking and bursting. The way in which the heat is applied and removed may affect the changes in the dimensions but most critical are the maximum temperatures employed.

Chemical and mineralogical composition

Fluxes produce glassy constituents in firing, while refractory constituents tend to keep the materials under fire in a resistant state. For pottery and enamelled metals the ware is invariably fired at temperatures much higher than those at which they will be used. Most tableware, for instance, is fired at 1000-1250°C but is used at room temperature. This is not so for other ceramics such as refractories. Thus, the minerals developed in a clay body during firing usually remain in the product for the rest of its life and are only important when they affect properties such as crazing resistance, thermal-shock resistance, strength and translucency. In the firing of glazes and enamels such minerals are important, for example, in producing crystalline and opacifying effects.

The way in which these minerals form in the ceramics is discussed below under 'Effect of heat on clays', and other headings.

28   EFFECT OF FIRING ATMOSPHERE

Pottery and enamels are fired in kilns and furnaces that use various fuels and power, including electricity, gas, coal, wood and oil. All such fuels need and produce an atmosphere inside the kiln. The effect of the atmosphere (see below) on the product being fired may be critical. The three types of atmosphere are neutral, oxidising (excess of oxygen) and reducing (lack of oxygen). The presence of absolutely clean heat in ceramic kilns is extremely rare and even with electrically fired kilns the products being fired usually succeed in contaminating the atmosphere. The dirtier the fuel, the greater the consideration needed.

29 DRYING PROCESSES

Before ceramics are fired they must be dried to remove the water that has been used to shape them. The water that can be removed by drying is called the *mechanical water* to distinguish it from the *chemical water* (water of constitution) that can be removed only by firing. Thus, the process of drying and firing are distinguished by the intensity of the heating.

The effects of drying clayware are 1. To evaporate the water in the ware and remove it as steam (causing loss in weight and build-up of pressure). 2. To cause the particles of clay and nonplastics making up the body to move together in a packing movement (shrinkage of the article, possibly leading to distortion). 3. To change the porosity (texture) and strength of the ware.

Applying the heat

The manner in which the heat is applied to the wet or damp clay is important. The three well-known methods are *radiation, conduction* and *convection*. In clayware drying, the design of drying equipment usually involves the use of combinations of these methods.

Effect of humidity

The rate at which the moisture leaves the ware depends on the humidity of the air surrounding it. If the air is saturated with moisture the steam in the drying clay will be unable to leave it and drying will effectively cease. The moist air must therefore be removed and replaced by drier air. Usually fans do this job but, in small workshops, opening a window will have a similar effect.

Drying rates

When clayware is allowed to dry in steady conditions of temperature, humidity and air velocity, it is found that the process of drying is split into two main stages, known as: (a) the constant rate period, and (b) the falling rate period.

Thus, in the first case the weight of the pot falls constantly with time, and at the end of say 10min drying under these conditions the weight lost would be double that lost after only 5min. In other words, loss in moisture is directly proportional to time. Under the falling rate period, however, the speed at which the moisture leaves the clayware decreases. In other words, in this period the drying rate depends directly on the amount of water left in the article and not on the time. A typical curve obtained by weighing drying pottery over a period of hours is shown in Fig 18.

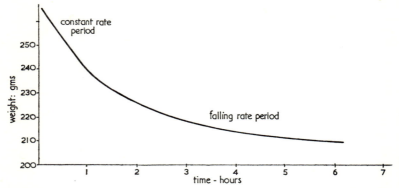

Fig 18 Curve showing how the weight of wet clay falls during the drying process. The terms 'constant rate' and 'falling rate' periods are explained in the text

The importance of these drying periods in practical potting is seen from a consideration of evaporation and steam pressure inside the ware. Towards the end of the falling rate period, the water has mostly left the pores of the clay and evaporation is no longer occurring merely at the surface of the clayware. In fact, the traces of water are evaporating *inside* the clay mass. The steam then has to diffuse through the channels of pores in order to escape. If it does not escape freely and steam pressure builds up, the inevitable result is damage to the ware in the form of cracking or even bursting.

The important factors in moisture diffusion are the density of the ware, its texture, porosity, temperature and humidity.

Surface moisture

Different types of clay exhibit different degrees of plasticity and also different sensitivities to drying. Clays absorb (surface sorption) different amounts of water on their particle surfaces. This is important in the drying of claywares, since it may need different lengths of time or different heating intensities to remove the final traces of moisture from the clays.

Bentonites (see Section 1), for example, are highly plastic materials with large proportions of colloidal material and high water-retaining powers. In certain humidity and temperature conditions bentonites absorb 10-15% moisture compared with only 1-5% for ballclays and about 0·5-1·5% for kaolins.

Drying shrinkage

A newly formed pot consists of a mixture of grains of non-plastics and plastics. The particles are surrounded by films of water. The nature and behaviour of these water films are very complex, involving the existence of forces of attraction, bound water, rigidly held water and bulk water—technical terms used by the rheologist to explain the peculiar behaviour of clay and water.

During drying, the films of water are removed, and the solid particles draw closer together. In other words, the clayware shrinks. The amount of shrinkage depends on many factors, including the nature of the clay, the particle sizes of the grains and the rate of heating.

The important practical point about clay contraction is that it must be made to occur within the strength limits of the article being dried, otherwise the article will be ruptured. In designing moulds and in modelling shapes, the potter must also pay attention to the contraction of the body so that the final size can be properly estimated.

A very important factor in clay drying is that the cessation of shrinkage does not mean that the ware is perfectly dry. The particles move together with drying but the last traces of moisture are removed after particle movement (and hence shrinkage) has stopped.

As soon as all the moisture has been removed from the clayware, the pores start filling up with air.

Leatherhard clay state

This is the condition in which shrinkage due to particle movement has ceased and the pores are filled with water. It is therefore a state reached before drying is complete. Many subsidiary shaping and embellishing operations (eg turning), call for the ware to be in the leather-hard (or cheese-hard) state, because it then has a greater toughness than in the absolutely dry state.

Drying the clay beyond the leather-hard state brings it closer to the *white hard* state, when it becomes brittle and very weak.

Practical points in drying

Artificial heat is not essential and many small workshops dry pottery by leaving it on open benches and shelves. The temperature of any hot air used must be controlled because of the danger of cracking. In casting, the plaster of Paris moulds are very adversely affected at 140°F (60°C). The plaster decomposes, the moulds lose their strength and crumble. If air circulation is used it must be uniform around the drying ware.

Hot surfaces will cause very rapid evaporation and, if new supplies of moisture coming from inside the ware cannot reach the surface to balance the loss through evaporation, cracking will occur.

Highly plastic clays and dense, very fine structured bodies dry more slowly and are more prone to distortion and warping than open, coarse-grained bodies. Grog will reduce shrinkage and keep the clay body straight (see Section 2). Flatware such as plates and plaques will dry faster than small dense articles such as vases. Stacking plates for drying converts them into a dense unit and drying will be slow. Cracking and warping in thrown pots may be due to strains formed during throwing, or to irregular distribution of water (poor skill). Ware left to dry near draughts may crack because the faster moving air will dry one side of the ware more quickly than the other and cause stresses in the clay.

Warping and cracking may also follow from anistropic shrinkage: different degrees of shrinkage in different directions on one piece of ware. Anisotropy may be due to the particle arrangement, the method of shaping, or the method of de-airing (pugging) the clay (see Section 2: Shaping).

Drying of cast pottery

Some of the water removed from casting slip, during casting up, leaves the pottery through the porous, absorbing mould. As soon as the slip is poured into the mould (see Casting), a thin layer of thickened clay forms on the plaster surface as a result of the flocculating (thickening) action of the calcium in the plaster. Water continues to leave the slip through the thin layer of clay which cannot shrink as long as it adheres to the mould. However, as soon as the stresses that are built up in this layer are great enough to overcome the forces making it cling to the mould, the clay parts from the mould. From then on, water removal can take place only by evaporation from the inside of the cast article (Fig 19).

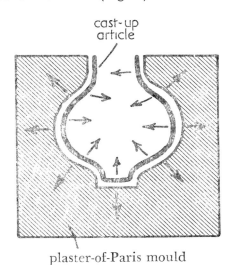

cast-up article

plaster-of-Paris mould

Fig 19 In slip casting water leaves the slip in two ways: through the absorbent plaster of the mould, and by evaporation. Soon after drainoff, the clay article pulls away from the mould and drying continues by evaporation only

In practice, about half of the water in casting slips is removed by the absorbent plaster mould, and the rest by evaporation. When ware is shaped by forcing plastic clay into
moulds, the mould removes about one-third of the moisture in
the clay and the rest is removed by evaporation.

30   ONCE OR TWICE FIRED?

The way in which glaze and body are fired has a critical effect on the quality of pottery. Some potters believe that by firing the clay first and then applying the glaze (the conventional industrial process of biscuit and glost firing), we kill the body. The only way to give a pot its full life is, they maintain, to fire all the raw materials together so that they react on each other to combine their most vital properties with the optimum effect. In practice this means shaping the clay and applying the glaze to the green pot, followed by a single firing, in which the body and skin mature together. Commercially, a compromise is reached—low biscuit temperatures, followed by high glost temperatures.

The outcome of once-firing is usually a thicker glaze with greater depth and character, a more highly developed intermediate layer (see Section 3) that gives a warmer glaze and an indefinable quality of 'one-ness' that comes from a sound marriage between glaze and body. Firing raw bodies and glazes together results in a fiercer reaction and better bonding between the materials.

Biscuit firing

This involves shaping the clayware, sponging and fettling and then stacking it densely in the kiln for firing. Since the ware is not fused (as in the firing of glazes), it can be placed in contact with other materials without danger of sticking. A wide range of temperatures is used for biscuit firing.

Earthenware and other similar porous bodies and also vitrified earthenware (hotel china, for instance) can be stacked in contact. Hollow-ware can simply be placed on kiln shelves.

Porcelain and bone china that will vitrify at the peak temperatures must be packed in a refractory powder (nowadays alumina, but in the past silica was used) which supports the softening body during firing and prevents distortion and twisting. Upon removal from the kiln the ware is brushed and is ready for decorating (underglaze) and dipping in the glaze.

Earthenware, which does not vitrify to the same extent as porcelain and bone china, can be freely placed without any support. In placing stacks of flatware such as plates and saucers, it is usual to sprinkle iron-free sand in the edge gaps to offer some support to the edges of the ware and hence keep them straight. After firing the earthenware biscuit is then brushed and goes for decorating and glazing.

The biscuit and glost firing techniques involved in this twice-fired process are aimed mainly at increasing the productivity of the factory. Biscuit kilns can be densely loaded with ware and, if the heating cycles are controlled by modern instrumentation, they turn out a standardised, uniformly fired product, one which according to some craft potters is absolutely lifeless, inert, and incapable of responding to the efforts of the glaze to bring warmth to the pottery as a whole.

Once-fired pottery

This is made by shaping the plastic clay and applying the glaze, followed by firing at a temperature high enough to mature the clay and glaze together.

Low-fired biscuit

This ware is frequently produced in some pottery making methods, (eg for stoneware) the aim being to give the clayware extra strength before glazing. The pots are then fired at the high temperatures used in the straight forward one-firing method. This technique gives some of the final effects of once-firing and has the advantage that the glazed ware placed for firing is mechanically much stronger. As the carbon matter has been removed together with the water of constitution (see page 182) the final firing can be done faster and with less danger to the ware.

Industrialised potteries first started to use the double-firing method because it can be employed to turn out a highly standardised product faster and more cheaply than the once-firing method. It was developed in England in the early 18th century and is commonly used in most industrialised countries of the world.

However, recent developments in faster firing and new kiln designs have made it feasible to once-fire certain items of mass-produced tableware, a move which may be seen as one back to the truly craft-potting technique, at least in theory. In practice, of course, the materials and firing process are so matched as to give a product identical in appearance with the twice-fired pot. Thus, the craft potter's wish to see raw glaze and raw body combined to produce living pottery is being thwarted. The reason is that all the life has been fritted out of the glaze and, with the fast-firing bodies now in use, there is little opportunity in the way of soaking time and temperature (heat work) for the essential reactions leading to the formation of a thick intermediate layer and the development of character in the glaze. Upon cooling, these once-fired wares are seen to consist of an inert body, carrying a thin, lifeless skin of glass.

To achieve the original once-fired effects of, say, the ancient Chinese potters, it would be necessary to apply raw glazes (ie unfritted) to the clayware and to refrain from excessive purification of the ceramic raw materials, both for body and glaze making. The final effect would be a less 'clinically pure' pot, with diffuse colouring, and a much thicker glaze whose warmth, due to its more highly developed intermediate layer, would be in evidence. It would be a less standardised article.

31 WHAT HAPPENS IN THE KILN?

The firing of pottery in a kiln is a complicated process involving many reactions, some of which have already been mentioned in Sections 1 and 3. Below, the effects of heat on the materials used in bodies, glazes and enamels are discussed in detail. However, firstly, here is a concise description of the firing process.

Dried clayware, when heated gently, first loses the traces of moisture adhering to the walls of the pores (up to temperatures of 200°C). Any carbonaceous matter, such as coal and lignin, starts to burn out, and some of the carbonates present decompose and lose their carbon dioxide. A common reaction is:

$$CaCO_3 \rightarrow CaO + CO_2$$

Thus, steam and gases leave the clay at this stage. As the temperature rises, the free silica in the body changes its crystal form. At about 460-540°C, the kaolinite (clay substances) starts to decompose and loses its water of crystallisation, thus sacrificing its plasticity. The kaolinite's crystal structure is broken down and it loses its orderedness in this process. Between 500° and 900°C other carbonates decompose and release fluxes into the body for reaction with the free silica and the components of the decomposed clay substance. At about 960°C, the decomposed kaolin may start to recrystallise, that is, to rearrange its molecules. Sometimes γ-alumina and even mullite are formed during these processes.

Once this point has been reached numerous ceramic reactions are occurring simultaneously. The feldspar or other main flux in the body begins to form glass which starts to attack the silica and clay particles, dissolving them, and as the temperature changes, precipitating other new minerals. The free silica remaining after the dissolving action also undergoes changes in its crystalline form (see below under Silica).

The results of all this decomposition, crystallisation, fusion, solution and inversion, once the article has been cooled, is the production of a hard, durable ceramic material. The types of minerals formed and the amount of glass present upon completion of the firing depend on the composition of the body and the firing temperatures reached.

Physical changes

Body changes after firing, apart from the obvious one that the clay has been converted to ceramic, include a change in the texture of the body. If the firing temperatures are only moderately high, the ware will be porous and absorbent. If a high temperature has been used, the body after firing will be dense, glassy and contain few pores.

It should be noted that very high temperatures are usually needed to make pottery bodies vitrify to absolute zero water absorption. It is rarely possible to make them absolutely without pores. High-fired porcelain and some stonewares may have an absorption of less than 0.5%, but the true porosity is still quite high. This apparently contradictory statement is due to the fact that inside the pottery body many of the pores are sealed and are not available for the transmission of moisture, that is, the body does not suck up the moisture. Nevertheless, the volume of pores in the body as a whole may be quite high (see Appendix 4).

High-temperature bodies

The compositions of bodies intended for high-temperature firing are different from those compiled to mature at low or medium temperatures. The difference lies mainly in the proportion of fluxing materials. Porcelain and some stonewares, for example, rely for vitrification mainly on the temperature, whereas vitrified earthenware relies on glass-forming oxides, added in large amounts to initiate fluxing at moderate temperatures.

Porcelains and similar high-temperature bodies contain a glassy matrix (about 50% of the volume) formed from the feldspar or Cornish stone. Mixes of other fluxes, such as wollastonite and calcium oxide, may also be used. Other minerals present include fused quartz and mullite. The latter, a highly stable, highly refractory (melting point 1810°C) compound, with the formula $3Al_2O_3.2SiO_2$, forms when kaolinite is decomposed and confers valuable properties on the ceramics. One such property is the high mechanical strength due to the entangled needle structure of the mullite.

Textural Changes in Firing

Early firing period	:	Very porous, as carbon burns out
Just before vitrification	:	Maximum porosity (very weak)
Vitrification starts	:	Glass begins to form and fill pores. Slowly, density increases, body **shrinks**

32 GLOST FIRING

In the kiln used to fire the glaze, the heat is applied in such a way as to fuse the glaze-forming materials applied to the body as a slip and make the resulting glass cover the surface of the ware in a smooth continuous coat. The molten glaze reacts with the surface layer of the body and upon cooling is attached to it.

When raw glazes are applied to clay bodies, that is, when none of the raw materials has been fired or fritted, the clay and glasses react more vigorously than when the clay has first been fired. For example, raw glaze will dissolve out a greater amount of iron from the body, thus discolouring itself, than would occur if the clay had been pre-fired (biscuited) and the glaze fritted. Raw glazes may dissolve certain constituents of the under-glaze colours, and cause discolouration of the glaze.

Once-fired pottery is therefore usually less white (for a given set of body and glaze materials) than twice fired. Non-fritted (raw) glazes react more readily with under-glaze colours and the pattern outlines may be more diffuse than if the decoration is applied to a biscuited body and then covered by a fritted glaze.

The net effect of biscuit firing and using fritted glazes, as discussed above, is to make the glaze and body less reactive to each other, to produce a sharper line between them, and to obtain thinner (cleaner) glaze films.

M

33 EFFECT OF HEAT ON CLAYS

Heat and clays are the two essential ingredients of pottery. The effect of one on the other has therefore been closely studied and the ceramist's research methods are so sophisticated that he can now produce a 'fingerprint' in the form of a heating curve for any type of clay. The technique known as *differential thermal analysis* (DTA) enables him to identify the minerals in clays, simply by heating a small sample of the clay with a reference material such as alumina and comparing the amounts of heat absorbed and emitted by the minerals as they are fired.

Some DTA curves for common clays are shown in Fig 20.

When the curve rises into a peak this means that heat has been produced by the minerals in the clay as they change their form or are decomposed (an exothermic reaction). On the other hand, the formation of a valley means that heat has been absorbed by the reaction (an endothermic effect). In this manner, it is possible to trace the heat needs of pottery bodies during the various stages of the firing process. The method is also used to indicate the presence, and even the amounts, of impurities.

When clays are heating the following reactions and effects occur: 1. Dehydration (loss of chemically combined water). 2. Phase changes (rearrangement of atoms in the crystals. 3. Oxidation of carbon (burning out of coal, wood, lignin, etc). 4. Vitrification (glass development). 5. Colour changes. (These depend on the colouring oxides present, eg Fe_2O_3 and TiO_2, and their state.)

Decomposition of kaolinite

In Section 1 it was stated that most common pottery clays

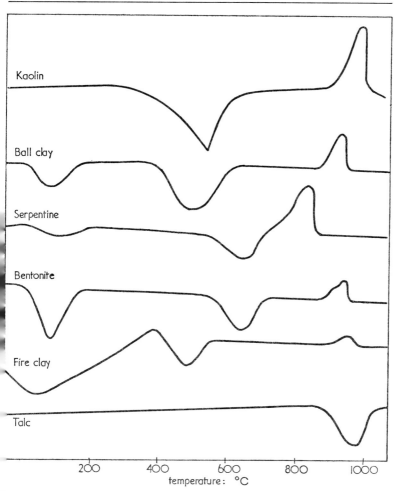

Kaolin

Ball clay

Serpentine

Bentonite

Fire clay

Talc

temperature: °C

ig 20 Differential heating curves (see text for definition) for some ommon clays and ceramic materials. These curves are a kind of 'inger print' for the materials and the technique of DTA is commonly used to recognise them

ontain large or small amounts of kaolinite. China clay is com-)osed almost entirely of this mineral and, because it is so im-)ortant to the potter and ceramist, they have learned a great .eal about it. When heated, kaolin (china clay) changes into metakaolin (having lost its water):

Kaolin   Metakaolin   Water

$$Al_2O_3.2SiO_2.2H_2O \rightarrow Al_2O_3.2SiO_2 + 2H_2O$$

As the temperature rises the metakaolin changes to spinel, and eventually to mullite. Silica is also formed with the spinel and the mullite.

In most pottery bodies the only reaction that occurs is the first one, that is, decomposition of the kaolinite to form metakaolin. This is because the other body ingredients begin to react with the metakaolin to form complex aluminosilicates and glasses. No mullite forms when earthenware is being fired. High-temperature clay bodies such as porcelain may produce some mullite. Metakaolin was once thought to be amorphous (ie not crystalline) because no pattern could be found in it by examining it with x-ray beams. However, it is now known that when kaolinite forms from heating kaolin it does indeed show signs of crystallisation, albeit very faintly.

Oxidation of clays in firing

This leads to the decomposition of sulphides and organic matter which are then removed as gases (SO_2 and CO_2, for example). The presence of varying amounts of oxygen in firing determines the colour of bodies and glazes, mainly because of the effects oxidation and reduction (lack of oxygen) have on the valency of colouring oxides present. For instance, iron is red when oxidised; it is then in the ferric state (Fe_2O_3); and blue-black when reduced [the ferrous state (FeO)]. If the clay vitrifies before all the carbon has been burnt out, the colour of the clay may be markedly affected and for large clay products, such as bricks, a black core may be found.

Sulphur in the form of sulphides and sulphates, if not removed during firing, may cause scumming and other 'soluble-salt' faults in the fired ware, making it difficult to glaze, and even causing bloating and blistering of clays upon refiring.

Vitrification

This has been mentioned above. Various clays have distinctive vitrification ranges, a term used to describe the temperature intervals over which a clay fuses. The temperatures at which clays start to vitrify depend on their composition and other properties. Vitrification in kaolinite and other clays can begin at temperatures below 900°C.

The completion of vitrification is *not* that state in which the clay has been changed to a glass. Vitrification is complete when the pottery can no longer be heated without distortion, warping or slumping. In practice, the point is recorded as being equivalent to a certain temperature but from the above we see that the time must also be taken into account.

Factors influencing the vitrification range in all types of clays are: 1. Rate of melt formation, which depends on the composition, especially the ratio of alumina and silica, and fluxing agents present (see Properties of Clays, Section 1). 2. Particle size of the minerals. 3. Heating rate.

Fireclays and kaolins may finally vitrify at very high temperatures (eg kaolins do so at 1600°C), but the range of temperature over which they vitrify may be quite short. On the other hand, some plastic clays may be fully vitrified at lower temperatures (as low as 1100°C for some stoneware clays and red-burning clays) but this state may be reached over a longer temperature interval.

In working out a firing cycle for a certain clay body, it is essential to know when the processes of vitrification start and finish. Only with this information is it possible to decide the appropriate maximum temperatures and soaking times.

The effects of vitrification are numerous: 1. The body shrinks. 2. Varying degrees of shrinkage occur. 3. Sometimes the body may expand or bloat. 4. Clay is converted to ceramic, ie from a friable into a hard, dense material. 5. The colour of the material changes. 6. The texture (porosity) alters.

34   HOW HEAT AFFECTS SILICA

Silica exists in three main forms, as quartz, cristobalite and tridymite. Some confusion often exists over the allotropic (crystal) modifications of silica. The purest form of silica is quartz. The shape of the crystal is externally hexagonal and corresponds roughly to a hexagonal form internally.

Alpha-Beta quartz

The arrangement of the atoms of silicon and oxygen making up the quartz crystal is complex at room temperature but when it is heated to 573°C the crystal suddenly expands and the atoms arrange themselves in a manner that corresponds to a simple hexagonal shape. The effect of heating to this temperature is to tidy up the arrangement of the atoms (straightening out the links).

Any pottery body containing raw (free) quartz will experience this rearrangement of its atoms when passing through the temperature of 573°C (either during heating or cooling).

The behaviour of silica when heated is very important to the potter. For example, in a mixture of free quartz and kaolin (the basis of many bodies) heated to about 600°C, two critical processes are occurring simultaneously: the quartz expansion with a volume change of about 1·5%, and the breaking down of the kaolinite molecule with the separation of water molecules (see above).

Thus, there is considerable movement in the body; it is weak, under stress, and prone to irregular heating. Should the temperature rise too quickly, or should steam be unable to escape from the body, cracking or even shattering may occur.

Quartz-cristobalite

A further rise in temperature to 870°C and above, causes another rearrangement to take place in the atoms of oxygen and silicon making up the quartz crystals. The quartz pattern is replaced by one known as 'cristobalite'. However, the change (from β-quartz to cristobalite) is very slow and occurs because the linkages between the atoms are not merely straightened, but broken, prior to rearrangement.

The conversion of quartz to cristobalite can be speeded up if certain mineralising agents are present, such as iron, soda and lime. Since a small amount of cristobalite is desirable in earthenware bodies (to enhance the crazing resistance—see below) the potter fosters its development in several ways: 1. Firing at high temperatures and soaking to give the quartz chance to convert. 2. The addition of lime to potter's flints during grinding so that the lime acts as a mineraliser for cristobalite formation. 3. Use of flint instead of sand, since the former changes more easily to cristobalite.

For the potter who uses stoneware and other fully vitrified bodies, the form of silica (sand or flint) used is not critical, since the properties developed in the body to make the glaze craze-resistant are different from those developed in porous earthenware bodies for that purpose.

In most pottery bodies fired at normal temperatures (below 1500°C) the silica is present either as quartz or cristobalite. However, silica can assume a third form, known as *tridymite*. In fact, researchers have now established that the three main forms of silica (quartz, cristobalite and tridymite) may exist in a total of at least eight forms (eg there are γ- and β-quartzes, γ- and β-cristobalite and various forms of tridymite).

TABLE 21
FORMS OF SILICA AND CRYSTAL CHANGES

| | | Practical Effects: | |
Temp.	Name of Change	In Firing	In Cooling
250°C	Alpha-beta cristobalite	3% sudden expansion	Sudden (3%) contraction (Glaze put in compression)
573°C	Alpha- to beta-quartz	1·5% sudden expansion	Sudden (1·5%) contraction (Glaze put in compression)
870°C	Quartz to cristobalite	Slow change; takes place over a wide temperature range	

For the potter needing to fire materials with the minimum of loss, most of the information available on silica transformations is only of theoretical interest. The most important changes in silica for the potter are shown in Table 21 with the accompanying practical effects.

Silica, crazing and cooling

The important silica changes taking place in the firing process also occur (in the opposite direction) during cooling. Two of these changes critically affect the crazing resistance of glazed ceramics. When the quartz in the body is changing from the beta- to the alpha-form upon cooling, it rearranges its atoms back into the slightly disordered state and shrinks. The effect of this quartz 'shrinkage' is to put the glass skin into compression (see Section 2). This state enhances crazing resistance.

A similar contraction occurs during cooling to 250°C when the cristobalite changes back into its low-temperature form. In practice the cooling of pottery through the above critical temperatures must be done carefully to avoid damage to the ware. It is the cooling of pottery below 650-680°C which is actually considered as the critical range.

In earthenware (porous) bodies, the cristobalite change on cooling is accompanied by a 3% contraction (much greater shrinkage than that taking place in the quartz changes at 573° C), and so is the more important of the two, since it is more effective in putting the glaze under compression.

Density changes in silica

The above silica conversions are accompanied by volume changes: the same numbers of atoms move about to occupy different amounts of space. This is expressed by saying that the material has changed its density (mass in a given volume of space).

The densities of the different forms of silica are quartz 2·65 gm/cm^3, cristobalite 2·33gm/cm^3, tridymite 2·27gm/cm^3, and fused glass 2·21gm/cm^3. From these figures we see that when one form changes into another there is inevitably some change in the space occupied (that is, in the specific gravity).

Practical firing procedure

The aim of the firing process should be to produce a durable ceramic body that retains its form and beauty for the maximum possible time. The technique is to apply the appropriate quantities of heat at the correct rates in order to bring about the desired changes in the body and glaze. If done properly, firing yields a mass of crystalline compounds bonded by a glassy matrix.

Inadequate heating will fail to produce enough glass and crystallisation, whereas excessive or too rapid heating may cause too much glass to form, or glass that is too fluid (glasses become more fluid as the temperature rises). Over-firing causes squatting, distortion and other faults. Underfiring means the ware lacks the 'ring' of a dense, crack-free body; it is too porous, soft, weak and will not last long in use.

Some craft potters, especially those who are highly productive and commercialised ignore the techniques that are needed to develop a dense, mechanically strong body. Since most bodies are glazed and coloured these potters seem to think that a low-temperature firing, sufficient to make the clay, silica and feldspar hold together until the glaze is in place, is good enough. Pottery made in this way lacks durability and loses much of the appeal of hand-potted ceramics derived only from high-temperature heat treatment.

Adding a lot of flux to the body to make it vitrify at a low temperature is no substitute for sound firing procedures.

35   REDUCTION AND OXIDATION

Simply, oxidation is the addition of oxygen. Thus, when iron and steel are allowed to become wet and are exposed to the air the subsequent process of rusting, in which the metallic iron acquires oxygen from the air, is known as oxidation. The metallic iron becomes an oxide and is said to have been oxidised. In ceramic firing, processes of oxidation are commonplace. Most ceramics and most metal enamels are fired in an oxidising atmosphere: with a copious air supply, so that all materials actively seeking oxygen can acquire it during the process.

Other examples of simple oxidation processes are the burning of sulphur to give sulphur dioxide; the burning of wood, coal and other fuels; and the explosion of petrol in an internal combustion engine.

In ceramic firing, however, when the materials are heated to very high temperatures the elements seeking oxygen may take it from compounds near at hand. In this case, oxidation involves removing oxygen from one compound by another, or by an element. For example, if magnesium ribbon is burnt in an atmosphere of carbon dioxide, the metal will take oxygen from the carbon dioxide, thus:

$$2Mg + CO_2 = 2MgO + C$$

The result of this combustion process is to form magnesium oxide by a process of oxidation. It will also be noted that the carbon dioxide, CO_2, has lost its oxygen and is therefore said to be reduced to carbon. The two processes occur together, in that if one substance is oxidised, another had been reduced.

Reduction processes

These are not so common in ceramics but they are important in obtaining special effects and if accidently obtained may cause faults. One classic example of reduction in ceramics is the production of copper red glazes, known as *sang de boeuf* and *rouge flambé* (see Section 3). Here copper oxide is reduced to the metal by a rather complicated reaction. In its oxidised state, as copper oxide, copper gives green-coloured glazes. Thus, reduction can bring about quite startling changes.

The way in which the ceramist oxidises or reduces his ware in firing is to provide an atmosphere in the kiln that is either plentifully supplied with oxygen, or short of it. In practice if reduction is called for, the supply of air is cut off or lessened and the fuel (gas, oil, solid) is allowed to burn with only a very small amount of air. If electricity is the power used for firing then it is necessary to add chemical agents that will produce the effect of robbing the ceramics of any oxygen they already possess.

For example, the inside of a saggar containing ware that is to be reduced may be made reducing by placing camphor (moth balls) in the saggar, which can then be sealed and fired in the usual (oxidising) kiln atmosphere. The atmosphere inside the saggar will become reducing as soon as the camphor is volatilised.

It is the environment that determines whether oxidising or reducing processes will occur. By 'environment' is meant not only the gaseous atmosphere inside the kiln or furnace, but also the mixtures of solids and fluxes that constitute ceramics and enamels. For instance, when thick clay ware is being fired, the early stages of the process are usually conducted in a strongly oxidising atmosphere, by feeding copious air into the kiln. This is to ensure that all the carbonaceous matter in the clay, and any sulphides, are burnt out, ie oxidised by oxygen in the air. The products of such combustion are removed as carbon dioxide and sulphur oxides.

However, if the carbon cannot get hold of enough oxygen from the kiln atmosphere it may take it from compounds in the clay. Another effect of oxygen starvation in such conditions would be the possible formation of black cores.

Iron compounds play a critical role in reduction-oxidation processes in the firing of ceramics. For example, iron oxides may produce low-fusing glasses if reduced, whereas, in the higher oxide states (ferric state as opposed to ferrous), they may be relatively inert. The colour of clay is dependent on the state of oxidation of the iron, and iron oxide has been called the most versatile of nature's pigments because of its ability to change the colour of its environment (see Section 3).

Reducing atmospheres in kilns may adversely affect the refractories and heating elements in the kiln, and potters considering the use of reducing fires should consult the supplier of the kiln about the possible effects. Special kilns can be provided for reduction using muffles, or, as mentioned above, saggars.

Oxidising and reducing agents

Oxidation and reduction are chemical reactions that depend on many conditions. What may be reducing in one case, may be oxidising in another. Usually oxidising agents are incorporated to provide a local supply of oxygen so that the reaction taking place in the body, glaze, or enamel is assured of oxygen at the critical stage and does not have to depend on the kiln atmosphere for a supply.

In the production of some ceramic colours, for instance, nitrates may be added to the recipe to do just this. Other oxidising agents are chlorates, dichromates, oxides of some metals; and for non-ceramic uses permanganates, nitric acid and aqua regia.

The main reducing agent used by the potter in firing is carbon monoxide. This is used indirectly by feeding excessive coal or natural gas to the kiln. Other examples of reducing agents are hydrogen, carbon (charcoal), carbon dioxide, ammonia and hydrogen sulphide. The use of hydrogen, for example, as a reducing agent is demonstrated by its action on copper oxide:

$$1. \quad CuO + H_2 = Cu + H_2O$$

The use of carbon monoxide as a reducing agent is illustrated by its action on ferric oxide (an important reaction in the blast-furnace smelting of iron):

$$2. \quad Fe_2O_3 + 3CO = 2Fe + 3CO_2$$

Perhaps the simplest method of producing a reducing fire, especially in electric kilns, is to drop lumps of charcoal in the kiln at the appropriate temperatures, taking care not to strike the ware. If gas is the fuel, it is quite easy to turn off the air supply and thus 'flood' the kiln with particles of unburnt carbon from the gas. These particles consume the remaining oxygen supply in the kiln and then start to take oxygen from the metallic oxides in the ware. However, no such technique is available to the user of electric kilns since these do not operate on combustion processes.

Special reducing kiln inserts are made by some kiln manufacturers (for instance, Podmore & Sons of Stoke-on-Trent). These 'bungs' are drilled to take a container that can be filled with pieces of charcoal. When the insert is replaced in the kiln wall it burns and gives the necessary reducing conditions.

In order to reduce colouring oxides (the commonest reason for using reducing firing) the gases must have access to the pigments. At temperatures below the setting point of the glazes, gases cannot permeate them, and so it is pointless creating reducing conditions after the glaze has solidified.

In practice, it is customary to start reducing after the maximum firing temperature has been reached and the ware is beginning to cool. A steady supply of reducing agent added to the kiln from the maximum heating point down to about 800°C should produce the desired reduced colour effects.

Some colours and glazes should not be reduced. Lead glazes, for example, are easily changed to black or grey, unattractive finishes even if only slightly reduced. The greyness is due to the formation of metallic lead.

In the reduction firing of some ceramic glazes, the ferric oxide is not reduced fully to the metal as shown in 2, but is only partly reduced. The reaction will thus be:

$$3. \quad Fe_2O_3 + CO = 2FeO + CO_2$$

Iron oxide in the Fe_2O_3 (ferric) state is red in colour. When reduced according to equation 3, to the ferrous state, FeO, it is blue or black. Thus, the reduction of iron oxide produces an important colour change.

It should be noted that in most craft potter's kilns the firing of reduced glazes involves considerable skill, since the control of the gas and air supply is a matter of judgement.

36 FIRING ENAMELS

When the enamel slip has been applied to the metal, as described in previous sections, the enamel is heated in a furnace at a temperature sufficiently high to fuse it and produce a smooth, stable, glassy coating.

During firing the particles of ground frits, clays, opacifiers, colourants and other inorganic materials in the slip, fuse together and form a single layer. Any organic agents that were added to make the unfired enamel coat stronger in handling will burn out during the early period of firing.

Firing conditions in enamelling determine the strength of adhesion (bonding) of enamel and metal and the finished appearance of the ware. To fire enamelled metal items they are placed on supports so that the fusing enamel does not cause them to stick to the bottom of the furnace or the staging. Items enamelled on only one side, of course, can be placed on the furnace shelf directly. Various articles of 'kiln furniture' made of heat-resistant steel, with points of contact kept sharp, are used in firing as supports. It is possible to reduce the dangers of sticking on the supports by coating them with kaolin wetted with water to form a slip.

The temperatures used to fire enamels depend on the composition of the enamel and the metal to which it is applied. Steel ground enamels for instance are fired at about 850°C and the enamel coats (the top decorative layer) at 800°-820°. Aluminium on the other hand is fired at a much lower temperature. Leadless enamels formulated especially for aluminium are usually fired at 550°-560°C for about 7-8 minutes. Copper, silver and gold enamelled wares are fired at 790°-810°C.

The firing times are much shorter than in the firing of ceramic glazes (seconds or minutes compared with hours or days), and there must be correspondingly greater control. Another important factor determined by the firing time is the propensity of the metal to distortion. Soaking or repeatedly firing a piece may weaken the metal base or cause distortion (see Fig 21).

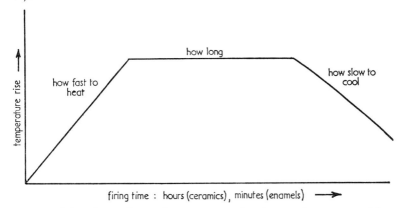

Fig 21   Firing depends on three stages: the time to heat up, soaking time or how long maximum temperature is maintained, and time taken to cool ware to room temperature

For steel articles carrying conventional enamels and a ground coat, the firing time at 1000°C would be 3-5 minutes for a metal thickness of 0·5mm. Increasing the metal thickness to 10-15mm would need the time to be increased to 20-40 min.

The bonding of enamel and metal and the various mechanisms responsible for this important aspect of the firing process are discussed in Section 2. Various types of reaction occur when the enamel fuses, for example, gas bubbling which may cause faults later.

Overfiring enamels is to be avoided. For instance, if ground enamels on steel are overfired, the glass enamel may become saturated with iron oxide from the metal; the usual fault following this is copper heading.

An indication that grounds have been overfired is the conversion of the normal black colour to a dirty green due to the presence of iron oxide. On the other hand, underfiring of grounds on steel causes the colour to remain blue-grey owing to the cobalt bonding agent, where this is used (sometimes nickel is used, and this symptom cannot then be used as an indication of firing efficiency).

Firing cover enamels

This is the most critical process of the enamelling craft and will decide whether the preceding processes have been done properly: mixing of frits, fusion, grinding and application and the matching of the frit to the particular metal.

The aim in firing the top coat is to achieve the optimum bonding with the ground coat (for steel) and the metal base for metals such as copper, aluminium and silver on to which no ground has been applied. In the final firing, any ground enamel already in place should soften so as to facilitate bonding with the top enamel, although the second firing may be taking place 30-50°C below the first firing.

Commercial suppliers of enamels formulate them to fuse and mature so as to yield the desired finish at certain firing temperatures. This information will be provided with the stock and the instructions should be carefully followed. The aim of firing is to develop brilliance and colour and to avoid boiling, blistering and other faults.

Underfiring, that is, using too low a temperature or too short a time, will cause the enamels to leave the kiln dull or matte.

Opacified enamels usually need a few minutes of 'soaking' after brilliance has been developed in order to give the crystals of opacifier time to form (see under opacification in Section 2).

Furnace atmosphere

Some of the principles of reduction and oxidation were mentioned early in this section. The effect of the furnace atmosphere is often critical in producing clean enamel. The presence of sulphur in the fuel used to be a serious problem in causing scumming (sulphates) and discolouration, and strongly reducing conditions may cause blackening of lead enamels. Thus, oxidising conditions should be carefully maintained in the firing of most enamels. Very 'wet' furnace atmospheres (above 3% water vapour) may produce rough grounds and blistered cover enamels.

37 FUELS AND COMBUSTION

A fuel is a substance containing carbon that will combine with oxygen to produce heat. Common fuels used in the firing of ceramics are wood, coal, peat, gas and oil. Electricity is a power source of heat but is not, under the above definition, a fuel, since no oxidation (combustion) is involved.

The contents of carbon in fuels are important and are determined by the time taken to form the fuel in the earth's crust. For example, anthracite coals were formed long before peat or lignite and this is shown up in their carbon contents. Anthracite contains about 95·5% carbon compared with 50% for wood, 59% for peat and 72% for lignite.

Combustion in ceramic firing processes is a chemical reaction and the products of that reaction (the gaseous atmosphere in the kiln) may have a critical effect on the ceramics being treated.

The potter faced with the choice of fuel wishes to know the kinds of effects produced by the various fuels available. In general, electricity is a very clean source of heating because no combustion products are formed, whereas fuel-oil may be considered to be a dirty fuel for the firing of fine ceramics, especially if it contains a lot of sulphur, which, upon combustion, produces sulphurous gases that may react with the ware and cause scumming and other faults. However, pure forms of oil are now marketed for clean oil firing.

Art potters have long ago recognised that wood-fired kilns produce softer, more interesting glazes than electric-fired or even gas-fired kilns. The effects obtained with wood are the subject of much controversy, but one undoubted cause of some of the pleasing effects is the chemically impure nature of the wood ash produced when wood is burnt in contact with clay.

N

Another factor is the long licking flames of burning wood and the manner in which these flames transfer their heat to the ware (gently and lovingly, as some potters would have it, compared with the harsh, staccatto bursts of the oil-fired burner in a large tunnel kiln).

Certainly the scientific explanations of combustion and heating cannot account for all of the artistic and highly desirable effects obtained by some craft potters through the use of wood firing.

It may be argued that heat is heat whichever form of fuel is used to generate it. But the time taken to produce heat, its intensity (temperature) and the presence of a particular chemical environment (ash-laden carbon monoxide, pure oxygen atmospheres, etc) will all modify the effects of the heat on the ware being fired.

Calorific value

Some fuels are 'stronger' than others in that a pound of one will produce more heat than the same weight of another. It is fairly obvious that a pound of firewood will produce less heat than a pound of anthracite coal when burned under the same conditions. The term 'calorific value' is used to express the number of heat units produced when a given mass of the fuel is burnt. The units of calorific value vary with the country: BTU's, therms, calories, and kilocalories are some units used in Britain, the USA, Europe and Asia.

Heat and temperature

Confusion sometimes arises in the use of these two words. Compare the heating of a steel rod in a fire with the boiling of a pint of water. The temperature of the red hot rod is much higher than the temperature of the boiling water, yet the latter probably contains more heat than the rod.

The property of temperature can be measured simply by one reading: on a thermometer or with special instruments discussed below. However, the measurement of heat requires a knowledge of the mass (weight) of the article, its specific heat, and its temperature. In fact, temperature can be said to be a measure of the intensity of the heat.

Heat, which is a form of energy, is due to the movement of

atoms and molecules in the material possessing the energy. As the temperature rises, the speed of the molecules rises. Simply, this is one of the reasons for chemical reactions taking place in clays and ceramics at high temperatures.

Flame temperature

When a fuel such as wood or dry grass is burned, flames are formed. The temperature of these flames is dependent on the type of fuel, that is, on the chemical composition and the calorific value of the fuel.

Primitive potters using grasses and brushwood cannot generate very high temperatures in their simple kilns because the maximum possible flame temperatures of their fuels are low. Industrial potters, however, using fuel oil and other high calorific fuels can produce very high temperatures (up to 2000°C) because of the nature of fuel oil, etc.

Among the types of fuels there is a hierarchy of flame temperatures, though other conditions such as the type of oxygen-carrier (combustion supporter) used, may have a bearing. For example, the flame temperatures of some gases are lower than that of fuel oil but, by using pure oxygen instead of air, it is possible to boost the flame temperature of the gas. This is because air contains 80% nitrogen that must also be heated before the essential job of heating and burning the oxygen and producing heat can be started.

Preheating the air before mixing it with the fuel for combustion is another method of raising the flame temperature.

The nature of the flames

Apart from their temperatures, flames have other important properties. The word *luminosity* is used to describe the light-emitting power of a flame; this depends on the fuel being burned and the combustion conditions such as the amount of air or oxygen and the thoroughness of mixing. The reader may be wondering how the luminosity of flames can affect the firing of clay and glazes. Since luminosity is due to the light-emitting behaviour of numerous tiny particles of unburnt carbon in the middle of the flame, it follows that the degree of luminosity is a measure of the carbon content of the flame. Now, as mentioned above, the carbon content of a kiln atmosphere and the way in which that atmosphere reacts with the clayware, can be very critical influences on the final product.

In some potteries the nature of the flames in a kiln is used as a method of controlling the firing process. Skilled potters estimate temperatures and atmospheric conditions by watching the flames. Luminosity is also important in the transfer of heat from flame to ware.

Draught

The burning of fuel requires oxygen, a gas that is usually obtained from air. Efficient combustion (minimum waste of heat) requires that the fuel and air be well mixed in the appropriate proportions. Draught is the technique used in pottery firing to bring about these conditions. It can be applied naturally (wind), by using chimneys or by using fans.

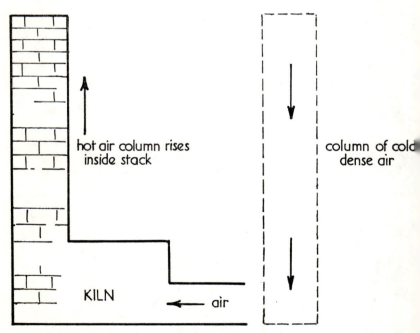

Fig 22 Principle of the kiln stack, showing how a draught is formed in a chimney, forcing air (oxygen) into the fireboxes and through the ware being fired. The hot air inside the kiln rises as the cold (and denser) air is forced downwards and into the firebox

If a stack of brushwood is ignited in the open, the oxygen in the immediate vicinity will be used up by combustion and the surrounding air will move in to take its place. This is a natural draught.

In kilns, the resistance to air movement may be so great (due to the setting density) that some aid must be provided to natural conditions so as to increase the force of the draught. If a stack or chimney is built over the fire, it is found that the pull of air through the fire and into the chimney is strengthened. The higher the chimney the stronger the draught, pulling fresh air over the flames.

If it is undesirable or impossible to build a tall chimney, mechanical fans can be used to move the air near the flames and force it into the combustion zone. In large kilns, air recirculating fans are commonly used to level out temperature differences.

In practice, the potter arranges a draught in order to speed up combustion by giving the flame more oxygen. It is necessary also to provide methods of increasing or reducing the draught. One such method is to use dampers, holes in the kiln wall or chimney that can be covered or partly covered, thus cutting down the intake of air.

38   TEMPERATURE MEASUREMENTS

The simplest and commonest method of measuring temperatures below the boiling point of water (100°C) is by noting the expansion and contraction of a thin column of mercury or other suitable liquid in a glass tube suitably marked with a scale. A wide range of such thermometers is available with different degrees of accuracy and marked with Centigrade (Celsius) and Fahrenheit scales. Steel-cased mercury thermometers can be used to measure temperatures of up to 600°C.

However, the ceramist needs to measure temperatures much higher than 600°C. Indeed, the range in which he is interested may be as great as 20-1500°C if he aspires to high-fired porcelain production. A glass-cased thermometer made to withstand even 360°C is obviously of no use for such temperatures.

Thermocouples are essential instruments for the potter who wishes to control his kilns by means other than human skill, trial and error and 'hoping for the best.' A thermocouple consists of a pair of metal wires fused together at the ends to make the *hot junction*. The other ends, (See Fig 23) are connected to the temperature indicator. The two wires are made of two

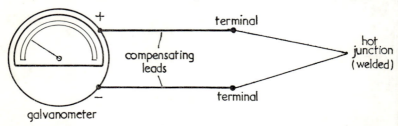

Fig 23   Principle of operation of a thermocouple. When the welded tip is heated a current flows in the wires and is recorded by the deflection of the galvanometer

different metals, such as platinum and an alloy of platinum and rhodium.

When the hot junction is heated in the flame, while the other ends are kept cold, a tiny electric current flows through the circuit, causing the needle in the indicator to be deflected. The higher the temperature difference between the hot and cold junctions of the wires, the stronger the current and hence the greater the deflection of the needle. Thus, the extent of the deflection can be used to measure the temperature of the hot junction and when this junction is placed in a kiln or furnace, it serves as a high-temperature indicator.

Other metal-wire combinations may be used. Table 22 shows the main combinations used in the pottery industry and the temperature ranges available.

TABLE 22

Type of Thermocouple	Temperature of Use
Platinum—13% Phodium/Platinum (noble)	Up to 1400°C
Chromel-Alumel (base metal)	Up to 1000°C
Iron/Constantan* (" ")	Up to 850°C
Copper/Constantan (" ")	Up to 400°C
*Constantan is a copper-nickel alloy.	

The hot junction of the thermocouple is a most delicate part of the circuit and it needs to be protected both from mechanical damage and the effect of adverse atmospheric conditions such as reducing gases inside the kiln or furnace. It is usual therefore to thread each separate wire on to porcelain or alumina 'beads' which insulate the wires from each other. This double row of beads is encased in a refractory sheath made from alumina or sillimanite. The sheath can then be inserted through a hole in the kiln wall into the kiln. The sheaths are usually 3-4 feet long.

Since the cold junction must remain cold, it is usual to connect the two wires of the thermocouple to base-metal, compensating leads so that the real cold junction can be moved away from the hot furnace walls. Care should be taken to ensure that positive is connected with positive, etc in the assembly of thermocouples with compensating leads.

After prolonged use at high temperatures, the welded tip of the hot junction (welding of the wires can be done by twisting the ends together and heating them with an oxy-acetylene torch) may deteriorate through alloy crystallisation, impairing the accuracy of the readings. Regular calibrations should therefore be carried out on thermocouples in use and the wires should be replaced when necessary. All noble-metal thermocouple wire should be returned to the suppliers since the metal can be re-used and some of the cost recovered.

Since the various metal and alloy combinations generate greatly different voltages, it is not possible to use different types of thermocouple without recalibrating the instrument recording the temperatures.

Thermocouples placed in a kiln will record the temperature of the spot in which the hot junction is located. Thus, several thermocouples will be needed if it is desired to obtain a complete pattern of temperature distribution in a large kiln.

Pyroscopes

These devices, which measure heat-work, are described in the Glossary, (See Fig 24).

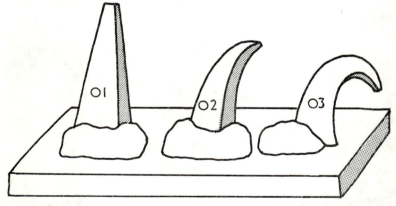

Fig 24 Pyroscopes (Seger cones) in firing. Cone 03 on the right has slumped, showing that the temperature in the kiln has reached at least 1040°C. The centre cone 02 (1060°C) is beginning to bend, while cone 01 (1080°C) still stands

Optical pyrometers

These are portable or fixed instruments that can be sighted on to a spot inside a furnace as a means of measuring tempera-

ture. The principle is that a wire is made to glow by passing a
current through it and then the brightness of this wire is compared with the brightness of the hot spot in the furnace. By
adjusting the brightness of the incandescent filament in the
instrument (by changing the current passing through it) until
it 'disappears' against the furnace background, we can read
off the temperature from a scale calibrated to show the relationship between current and temperature.

39   KILN REFRACTORIES

The design of pottery kilns and enamelling furnaces is outside the scope of this book. The types of refractory (heat-resistant) materials used in building up the shelves inside kilns can be briefly mentioned.

Refractories used in furnaces and kiln buildings are made from a wide range of materials by plastic shaping, casting and pressing, followed by firing at high temperatures to develop the mechanical strength, heat resistance and other properties required for use at pottery firing temperatures.

Fireclay Refractories are commonly used. The quality is usually dependent on the alumina content of the raw materials, a common range containing 35-37% alumina.

Sillimanite refractories made from sillimanite minerals such as andalusite and kyanite (the general formula of the group is $Al_2O_3.SiO_2$), contain about 60% alumina and are excellent materials for bats, slabs and supports for use in kilns and on kiln cars.

The essential property of all kiln furniture is the ability to withstand repeated heated and cooling when subjected to high temperatures under load. Other important properties are the ability not to contaminate or stick to the product being fired, and good spalling (thermal-shock) resistance.

Silicon carbide, bonded with clay or nitrides, is also an excellent material for kiln furniture because of its high refractoriness-under-load. In glost kilns the setting of the glazed ware necessitates the use of supports that must not stick to the fusing glaze. By building up assemblies of pillars, suitably perforated to carry ancillary supports, the glost placer can ensure that glazed flatware is suspended with only the minimum of contact. Use is made of cranks, posts, saddles, spurs, stilts and pins—all made of refractory materials.

To prevent the ware sticking to kiln furniture it is a good plan to coat the latter with a kaolin wash or a mixture of kaolin and zircon before use. These materials are not readily wetted by the fusing glaze and this helps to keep ware and furniture apart (See Page 150).

section 5

GLOSSARY OF PROCESSES AND MATERIALS

APPENDIX 1   CHEMICAL FORMULAE OF CLAYS AND GLAZES

To understand clays, glazes, enamels and pigments, one must be familiar with chemical symbols, formulae and equations. The formation of kaolin, for example, the foundation stone of the potter's craft, can be followed only through the chemistry involved in the statement: feldspar is broken down by acid to yield kaolinite, silica and potash. The formula and its interpretation are discussed below. The mixing of glazes and enamels is possible only by reference to chemical formulae, especially if technical sources are used for the recipes.

Clay analysis

When the ceramist states that a chemical analysis of a certain clay shows that it contains 45% of silica, (written: 45% SiO_2), he means that in each 100 parts by weight of the clay there are 45 parts by weight of the chemical compound, silicon dioxide, which has the formula SiO_2.

The analysis is recorded as a list of *oxides* and gives the contents of each oxide in percentages. Simply by knowing the properties of these ceramic oxides and reading an analysis, a potter can often predict how a given clay or raw material will behave in moulding and firing, though many other pieces of information are needed to support such a prediction. Some chemical analyses of common clays are given in Table 1.

Glass, frit and glaze analysis

A chemical analysis of an enamel or a glaze indicates the concentrations of oxides. By comparing the analysis with that of other frits or enamels it is possible to get some idea of their relevant behaviour. However, since the melting of glasses is a complex process (see Section 2), the ceramist uses a much more effective type of formula, known as the *molecular* or *Seger* formula, discussed below.

Elements and atomic weights

Appendix 2 shows a list of all the chemical elements of value to the potter and enameller. Also given are the atomic weights and the symbols of the elements. For instance hydrogen is denoted by Hydrogen, H, 1.

By comparing the weights of all other elements with hydrogen, whose atomic weight has been fixed as one, we can give numbers to all other elements. Thus one atom of oxygen is sixteen times heavier than one atom of hydrogen, so we say that the atomic weight of oxygen is 16. And so on.

Molecular weight

When atoms combine they form molecules. Thus, one atom of silicon will join itself to two atoms of oxygen to form a compound known as silicon dioxide. The potter knows it as silica, quartz, sand and potter's flint. This compound has the formula SiO_2, and the way it is written indicates that one silicon atom is joined to two oxygen atoms. By adding together the weights of all the atoms in this molecule of silicon dioxide we find its molecular weight:

$$28 \quad + \quad (2 \times 16) \quad = \quad 60$$
$$Si \quad + \quad O_2 \quad = \quad SiO_2$$

Appendix 3 shows a list of all the important compounds used in ceramics together with their molecular weights. Here are three other examples.

1. Fe_2O_3 : two atoms of iron (Fe) and three atoms of oxygen (O)

$$(2 \times 56) \quad + \quad (3 \times 16)$$
$$112 \quad + \quad 48 \quad \quad = \quad 160.$$

2. Al_2O_3 : two atoms of aluminium and three of oxygen

$$(2 \times 27) \quad + \quad (3 \times 16)$$
$$54 \quad + \quad 48 \quad \quad = \quad 102.$$

3. $Na_2B_4O_7$: two atoms of sodium, four of boron, seven of oxygen

$$(2 \times 23) \quad + \quad (4 \times 11) \quad + \quad (7 \times 16)$$
$$46 \quad + \quad 44 \quad + \quad 112 \quad = \quad 202.$$

Sometimes a formula will contain several molecule groups joined by a full stop, thus:

4. $Na_2B_4O_7.10H_2O$.

This means that in addition to the atoms shown in example 3 there are ten molecules of water (H_2O). If the figure appears in front of the molecule, as here ($10H_2O$), it means that the molecular weight must be multiplied by that figure, thus:

$$Na_2B_4O_7.10H_2O = 202 + 10 \ (2 + 16)$$
$$202 + 10 \ (18)$$
$$202 + 180 = 382$$

Let us use the above simple arithmetic to interprete the meaning of the statement that clay is formed when feldspar is broken down by acid to give kaolinite, silica and potash. It can be represented as a set of formulae joined to form a *chemical equation*.

5. $K_2O.Al_2O_3.6SiO_2 + 2H_2O + CO_2$
$Al_2O_3.2SiO_2.2H_2O + K_2CO_3 + 4SiO_2$

This appears highly complicated, but if we examine each molecular group in exactly the same way as we did for the above examples, a clear understanding of the principles of molecular formulae in pottery and ceramics will evolve.

Feldspar has the formula $K_2O.Al_2O_3.6SiO_2$. This is the first group in equation 5. Its molecular weight, worked out by adding up the atomic weights as shown above comes to 556. The second group is $2H_2O$ which simply means that there are two molecules of water. The third group is CO_2 which stands for one molecule of carbon dioxide (the molecular weight of CO_2 is $12 + (2 \times 16) = 44$). As there are two molecules, the 'weight' of carbon dioxide here is 88.

Now when the above three substances react, as they did in the earth's crust when clays were being formed from granite, the substances represented on the right-hand side of the equation were produced. The arrow is a chemical shorthand symbol indicating that a reaction has occurred. Sometimes the equation sign ($=$) is used.

Examining the right-hand side of the equation, we see that the new substances are:

Kaolinite, with the formula $Al_2O_3.2SiO_2.2H_2O$ (molecular weight): $102 + 2(60) + 2(18) = 258$.

P

Potash (potassium carbonate) with the formula K_2CO_3 (molecular weight 138).

Silica (silicon dioxide) with the formula SiO_2 (molecular weight 60).

If we add up all the atomic weights on the left-hand side of the equation, the total should be the same as the sum of the atomic weights on the right-hand side, that is, the equation is said to balance. Note, however, that the *numbers of molecules* are not balanced: we start with one molecule of feldspar, two of water and one of carbon dioxide. But we finish up with one of kaolinite, one of potash and four of silica. Thus

Starting Materials

1 Feldspar + 2 water + 1 carbon dioxide

$$556 + 2(18) + 44 \qquad\qquad = 636$$

Products

1 Kaolinite + 1 Potash + 4 Silica

$$258 + 138 + 4(60) \qquad\qquad = 636$$

The fact that the equation is balanced indicates that all the atoms with which we started are accounted for in the products with which we finished. This is an important principle in ceramic calculations, especially in using molecular formulae in glaze arithmetic.

Glaze calculations

In mixing the glaze, the potter uses various recipes indicating 'parts by weight' of raw materials and frits. Providing these starting materials are pure chemical compounds, there is no difficulty about producing the desired results. However, glaze-making materials include clays, feldspars and frits that are variable in composition, and so some standardised method of handling glaze compilation is used: a method that produces satisfactory results regardless of the variations in the raw materials.

One standardised method of recording glaze formulae is in the form of percentage parts of the oxides present in the fired glaze. This can be obtained simply by making a chemical analysis of the glaze. An example of the result would be 64·2% PbO, 5·8% Al_2O_3, and 30·0% SiO_2.

This is an analysis for a simple lead silicate glaze or frit. However, by going a stage further and arranging this oxide formula into a molecular formula, it is possible to make all glaze formulae comparable, regardless of the starting materials. The molecular formula method was originated by Hermann Seger who gave his name to the technique, one that is widely used in glaze calculations, although in some countries it is still common practice merely to report the glaze formula as the oxide percentage.

Calculating molecular formula from percentage oxides

A full chemical analysis of kaolin (china clay) shows that it contains 46.5% SiO_2, 39.5% Al_2O_3 and 14.0% H_2O. By dividing each oxide percentage by the molecular weight (see above), we obtain the molecular parts, thus:

%		MW		Mol Parts		Ratio
46.5	÷	60	=	0.775	SiO_2	2
39.5	÷	102	=	0.387	Al_2O_3	1
14.0	÷	18	=	0.777	H_2O	2

Now the ratio of these molecular parts is found to be 2 : 1 : 2 (divide each by the smallest number, ie 0.387). Thus the molecular formula of kaolin is $1Al_2O_3.2SiO_2.2H_2O$. Normally, we omit the figure 1 in front of Al_2O_3. Conversely, the oxide percentages are found by multiplying the molecular parts by the molecular weights.

Sum of bases must equal one

In using the Seger formula, it is the practice to report the bases (CaO, PbO, etc) in a single column and to make them add up to one. This makes all molecular formulae comparable and enables us to predict certain important properties of a glaze merely by looking at its formula. An example will illustrate the arithmetic behind this principle, (see also Page 120).

Lead silicate frit formula

A commercial lead frit upon analysis is found to contain 65% PbO, 2.7% Al_2O_3 and 32.3% SiO_2. Following the procedure of the previous section, we obtain

Oxide %		MW		Mol Parts		Ratio
65	÷	223	=	0.29	PbO	1.00
22.7	÷	102	=	0.027	Al_2O_3	0.100
32.3	÷	60	=	0.538	SiO_2	1.855

Here we use the basic oxide PbO as the unifying factor, and divide throughout by 0·29. The answers are given in the ratio column. Thus the molecular or Seger formula of this lead frit is PbO 0·1Al$_2$O$_3$ 1·855SiO$_2$. Incidentally, the three columns thus formed are invariably in this order : bases, amphoteric and acid.

From the oxide analysis of any glaze it is possible to calculate the molecular formula in this way, that is, by dividing each oxide percentage by the molecular weight and arranging the result so that the bases equal unity, (ie add up to one).

In technical literature the potter or enameller may come across a glaze or frit formula that he decides will suit his conditions. How is the molecular (Seger) formula converted into a workable recipe? First, here is a simple example, for a pure chemical compound, to illustrate the principle.

Calculate the percentage composition of whiting, CaCO$_3$, in terms of CaO and CO$_2$

When heated CaCO$_3$ changes to CaO + CO$_2$. The molecular weight of CaCO$_3$ is 100 (see above).

$$\text{Calcium Oxide CaO}: \quad \frac{56 \times 100}{100} \quad = \quad 56\%$$

$$\text{Carbon dioxide CO}_2: \quad \frac{44 \times 100}{100} \quad = \quad 44\%$$

Thus, the percentage composition of whiting is 56% CaO and 44% CO$_2$. In other words every 100gm of whiting, when fired, produces 56gm of CaO, while the rest is removed as carbon-dioxide gas.

Formula to percentage oxide

Now let us use the above arithmetical principles to convert an actual glaze formula into a percentage oxide formula.

1. Seger formula is: 0·6PbO ⎫
                      0·3Na$_2$O ⎬ 0·24Al$_2$O$_3$ 2·0SiO$_2$ O·4B$_2$O$_3$
                      0·1CaO ⎭

To calculate the percentage oxide composition

PbO	0·6	x 223	=	133·8
Na₂O	0·3	x 62	=	18·6
CaO	0·1	x 56	=	5·6
Al₂O₃	0·24 x 102		=	24·5
SiO₂	2·0	x 60	=	120·0
B₂O₃	0·4	x 70	=	28·0
				330·5

That is, 330·5 is the formula weight of the glaze. We now convert the results obtained to the approximate percentage oxide composition by multiplying by $\frac{100}{330·5}$. Thus, we get:

PbO	40·54%
Na₂O	5·63%
CaO	1·70%
Al₂O₃	7·42%
SiO₂	36·36%
B₂O₃	8·50%
	100·15%

Converting glaze formulae to recipes

The stages in producing a workable recipe expressed in parts by weight of raw materials are: 1. Seger formula of glaze (given). 2. Calculation of the Seger formulae of the raw materials from the oxide formula. 3. Converting to recipe.

The molecular formulae of many common materials have been worked out and are quoted in Appendix 3. For example, the molecular formula of china clay, as already shown, is $Al_2O_3.2SiO_2.2H_2O$; that of potash feldspar is $K_2O.Al_2O_3.6SiO_2$.

However, apart from relatively pure natural materials such as flints, quartz sand, china clay and also chemical compounds such as whiting, potassium carbonate, borax and various colouring oxides, such as cobalt oxide and manganese dioxide, it is rarely possible to use standardised molecular formulae. It is necessary to analyse the materials, obtain an oxide formula and then work out the molecular formula as described above.

Example: Calculate a working recipe from the following glaze formula:

$$\left.\begin{array}{l} 0.40\text{K}_2\text{O} \\ 0{\cdot}50\text{PbO} \\ 0{\cdot}10\text{CaO} \end{array}\right\} \qquad 0{\cdot}40\text{Al}_2\text{O}_3 \qquad 3{\cdot}6\text{SiO}_2$$

Note that the bases add up to one. The first question to be answered is: which raw materials are to be used? By examining the formulae of the glaze and the glaze-making materials, the potter selects a number of raw materials (or raw materials and frits) which when blended and fired will yield a glaze corresponding to the starting formula. This, after all, is the whole purpose of using molecular formulae in glaze compilation. Obviously, all the oxides named in the molecular (Seger) formula must be available from the collection of raw materials.

Which raw materials are available? The various ceramic raw materials and the oxides they contribute to glaze making are discussed in Section 2. Here, let us assume that for our formula we have decided upon: feldspar, whiting, lead bisilicate frit and sand. The chemical analysis (or molecular formulae) of these starting materials, show that they contribute the following oxides: K_2O, PbO, CaO, SiO_2 and Al_2O_3, that is, all the oxides given in the molecular formula. Furthermore these materials do not contain any oxides not mentioned in the formula. For instance, a possible source of calcium oxide is dolomite but this would also bring in MgO, which is not desired for this particular formula. Thus dolomite cannot be used. On the other hand, it is possible to find other suitable materials, e.g. Cornish stone or nepheline syenite instead of feldspar, and potter's flint (SiO_2) in place of the sand.

Red lead or white lead can be used to contribute lead, PbO, but these are raw lead forms and their use is restricted for health reasons. The lead is usually used in the form of frits.

In converting a formula to a recipe it is advisable to draw up a table, thus:

Material	Molecular Weight	Molecular Parts	Parts by weight	K_2O	PbO	CaO	Al_2O_3	SiO_2
Feldspar	556	0.40	222.4	0.4	—	—	0.4	2.4
Whiting	100	0.10	10	—	—	0.1	—	—
Sand	60	0.20	12	—	—	—	—	0.2
Lead Frit	343	0.50	172.5	—	0.5	—	—	—

Feldspar's formula:	$K_2O\ Al_2O_3\ 6SiO_2$
Whiting's "	$CaCO_3$
Sand's "	SiO_2
Lead frit's "	$PbO.2SiO_2$

The 'Parts by weight' column, is deduced by multiplying the 'molecular weight' by the 'molecular parts' and it gives the final recipe. Thus our recipe in parts by weight is

222·4	Feldspar
10·0	Whiting
12·0	Sand
172·5	Lead frit

Interpretation of the above table

The amounts of raw materials must be selected to yield the molecular parts stated in the Seger formula. Thus, 0·40 molecular parts of feldspar yields $0·4K_2O$, $0·4Al_2O_3$ and $2·4SiO_2$ (ratio 1 : 1 : 6). Similarly, 0·10 parts of whiting yields $0·10CaO$, and 0·20 parts of sand gives $0·2SiO_2$. Finally, 0·50 molecular parts of lead frit yields $0·5PbO$ and $1·0SiO_2$ (ratio 1.2). by adding up the columns we arrive at the original molecular formula: viz $0·4K_2O$, $0·5PbO$, $0·1CaO$, $0·4Al_2O_3$ and $3·6SiO_2$.

It should be noted that the amounts of such materials as sand (flint) and calcium carbonate, will be determined by the balance required after a decision has been made as to how much feldspar etc has been added. Since some materials contribute more than one oxide, these must be dealt with first. In the above example, the sand is left till the end. We find that the feldspar gives $2·4SiO_2$ and the frit $1·0SiO_2$, making 3·4 SiO_2; thus the sand must give the balance of $(3·6-3·4) = 0·2SiO_2$.

Calculating recipe to formula

Any glaze recipe can be expressed as a molecular formula using the principles outlined above. The procedure is simply that of reversing the stages, using the data given in the appendices for molecular formulae, molecular weights, etc. Naturally, the more complex the formulae and the greater the numbers of oxides present in the materials, the more arithmetic involved.

This particular kind of calculation is very useful to potters who may have received recipes in the form of percentage weights of raw materials and who, knowing the analyses of those raw materials, wish to work out the Seger formula of the glaze in order to compare it to their glazes.

APPENDIX 2   CHEMICAL ELEMENTS AND ATOMIC WEIGHTS

Element	Symbol	Atomic Weight	Element	Symbol	Atomic Weight
Aluminium	Al	27	Manganese	Mn	55
Antimony	Sb	122	Molybdenum	Mo	96
Barium	Ba	137	Nickel	Ni	59
Beryllium	Be	9	Oxygen	O	16
Bismuth	Bi	209	Phosphorus	P	31
Boron	B	11	Platinum	Pt	195
Cadmium	Cd	112	Potassium	K	39
Cesium	Cs	133	Scandium	Sc	45
Calcium	Ca	40	Selenium	Se	79
Carbon	C	12	Silicon	Si	28
Cerium	Ce	140	Silver	Ag	108
Chlorine	Cl	35	Sodium	Na	23
Chromium	Cr	52	Strontium	Sr	88
Cobalt	Co	59	Sulphur	S	32
Copper	Cu	63	Tin	Sn	119
Fluorine	F	19	Titanium	Ti	48
Gold	Au	197	Tungsten	W	184
Hafnium	Hf	179	Uranium	U	238
Hydrogen	H	1	Vanadium	V	51
Iron	Fe	59	Yttrium	Y	89
Lead	Pb	207	Zinc	Zn	65
Lithium	Li	7	Zirconium	Zr	91
Magnesium	Mg	24			

APPENDIX 3 SOME CERAMIC MATERIALS AND THEIR MOLECULAR WEIGHTS

Material	Formula	Molecular Weight
Albite (soda feldspar)	$Na_2O.Al_2O_3.6SiO_2$	524
Anorthite (lime feldspar)	$CaO.Al_2O_3.2SiO_2$	278
Borax, hydrated	$Na_2B_4O_7.10H_2O$	381
Boracite (mineral)	$6MgO.MgCl_2.8B_2O_3$	—
Borocalcite	$CaO.2B_2O_3.6H_2O$	—
China clay (kaolin)	$Al_2O_3.2SiO_2.2H_2O$	258
Cryolite	$3NaF.AlF_3$	210
Dolomite	$CaCO_3.MgCO_3$	184
Feldspar (lime)	see anorthite	—
Feldspar (potash)	$K_2O.Al_2O_3.6SiO_2$	556
Feldspar (soda)	see albite	—
Gypsum	$CaSO_4.2H_2O$	172
Ilmenite	$FeO.TiO_2$	156
Lead bisilicate (frit)	$PbO.2SiO_2$ (usually contains Al_2O_3)	343
Nepheline syenite	Nepheline plus feldspar	—
Nepheline (mineral)	$K_2O.3Na_2O.4Al_2O_3.8SiO_2$	—
Petalite	$Li_2O.Al_2O_3.8SiO_2$	612
Sodium carbonate (soda ash)	Na_2CO_3	106
Spodumene	$Li_2O.Al_2O_3.4SiO_2$	372
White lead (basic lead carbonate)	$2PbCO_3.Pb(OH)_2$	776
Wollastonite	$CaO.SiO_2$	—
Zircon	$ZrSiO_4$	183
Zirconia	ZrO_2	123

APPENDIX 4   USEFUL FORMULAE

Density

Density, specific gravity and bulk density are terms frequently used in describing ceramic bodies, metals and raw materials. Density is the amount of mass in a certain amount of space. Density is mass in unit volume, and can be written as

$$D = \frac{Mass}{Volume}$$

For our purpose, mass is equivalent to weight. Thus, the mass of a lump of plastic clay is, like its weight, measured in grams, pounds, or ounces. Let us take a common example. If a pint of casting slip is found to weigh 36oz, we say that the pint weight is 36oz. The unit of this measurement is oz/pint, which is equivalent to reporting it as:

$$PW = \frac{Mass}{Volume} \text{ or } \frac{(Weight)}{(Pint)}$$

Thus, pint weight is a measure of density.

Outside Britain and the USA, the density of casting slips may be measured in terms of grams per litre. This, too, is a measurement of density, since

$$\frac{Grams}{Litre} = \frac{Mass}{Volume} = Density$$

Specific gravity

In order to standardise measurements it is convenient to use definitions that are valid regardless of the units of weight (mass). By comparing the densities of materials such as clay, metals, wood, ceramic and concrete with a common substance, like water, it is possible to obtain such standardisation and to get a clear idea about the relative properties of these materials. The question asked is 'how many times is the density of the material greater than that of water?' In other words, the density of water is used as the reference point. By comparing the densities of all materials with the density of water, we can then compare the density of any of those materials with the others. Thus, specific gravity is defined as

$$\frac{\text{Density of the material}}{\text{Density of the water}}$$

Now, the density of water is found to be 1 gram per cubic centimetre (or $1\text{gm}/\text{cm}^3$, also written as $1\text{gm}/\text{ml}$ which stands for millilitre. This is simply because $1,000\text{gm}$ of water at a given temperature occupy one litre of space).

Since the division by the figure 1 leaves the density of the material unaltered, we see that the specific gravity of a substance is numerically the same as the density. The important difference is that it is not necessary to quote the units (gm/cm^3 etc) when reporting specific gravity. In other words, the specific gravity or relative density, as it is sometimes called, is merely a ratio.

Most ceramic materials, even glazes and glasses, contain pores—tiny holes arranged in various ways to form honeycombed structures. These pore systems may allow gases and liquids to enter the ceramics, and so they are important in considering the way the ceramics are to be used. Now, some of the pores may be sealed by the glassy material in the body. Other pores will be open, forming communication channels through the body. The relative proportions of 'open' and 'closed' pores are therefore important.

Some definitions relating to volumes, density and porosity will be useful to the potter.

Bulk volume

This covers the apparent volume occupied by a porous solid article such as a clay tile or a brick. It can be measured simply by measuring the dimensions. For instance, a clay block measuring $2 \times 4 \times 9\text{cm}$ would have a volume of 72 cubic centimetres. In other words, this clay block takes up 72cm³ of space or volume.

True volume

For porous solids, such as a fired brick or earthenware pot, the bulk volume defined above, includes the solids and the pores in the article. In order to find the true volume, we must eliminate the pores and measure the volume occupied by the solids alone. Obviously, the true volume is less than the bulk (its apparent) volume. One method is to grind up the brick or clay article very fine and measure the volume occupied by the resulting powder, free of pores.

Bulk and true densities

By using the weights (masses) of the brick and tiles, together with the bulk volume and true volume as defined above, we can obtain the bulk and true densities from the equations:

$$\text{Bulk Density} = \frac{\text{Weight}}{\text{Bulk Volume}}$$

$$\text{True Density} = \frac{\text{Weight}}{\text{True Volume}}$$

In practical precise determinations, a third complicating factor (the apparent solid volume) has to be considered because in real measurements we cannot easily take account of the sealed pores that remain even in tiny grains of crushed brick, clay, etc.

Porosity

The porosity of ceramics is usually expressed as a 'percentage'. It is determined by comparing the volume or space occupied by the pores with the space occupied by the ceramic article as a whole. In other words, the greater the volume of pores in a brick, say, then the higher its percentage porosity. As we reduce the percentage porosity, we make the brick denser.

Practical measurements involve difficulties for the reasons mentioned above: we must consider the sealed pores as well as the open pores.

Water absorption

A simple method of giving an indication of the porosity of a fired pot is to measure the volume of water (or in practice the weight of water) soaked up when the article is immersed in water. For vitrified materials, it is usual to boil the test pieces in water for about an hour and then carefully dab off the excess moisture and weigh them. The difference in the weights before and after soaking indicates the amount of water absorbed into the pores of the article. This is a very useful indication of the degree of vitrification of many common pottery bodies. Obviously the greater the glass formation, that is, the higher the degree of vitrification, the less will be the porosity of the article and the less will be the absorbed moisture.

In precise measurements, accurate definitions, taking into account the above difficulties, are recorded for apparent porosity and true porosity. The true porosity, for example, takes into account the total pores, both open and closed, in determining the proportion of pores relative to the real volume of the article.

Slip formula

It is often desired to calculate the amount of solids in clay or glaze suspensions. Obviously in a given volume of slip, for instance a pint, some of the space is taken up by water. The problem is to decide how much of the pint weight is contributed by the solids and how much by the water. The solution to this problem can be obtained by using a simple formula known as *Brongniart's Formula*. This is written as:

$$W = (P - 20)\ \frac{SG}{SG - 1}$$

Where W is the weight of solids in the volume of slip,

$$P = \text{its pint weight}$$
$$SG = \text{the specific gravity of the solids in the slip.}$$
$$20 = \text{the weight in ounces of a pint of water.}$$

Thus, for instance it is found that the pint weight of a casting clip is 36oz. Find the actual weight of solids in this volume.

From the above formula

$$W = (36 - 20)\ \frac{SG}{SG - 1}$$

It is usual to consider that the specific gravity of a common earthenware slip is 2·5, thus the answer to the above problem is

$$W = (16)\ \frac{2·5}{1·5}$$

$$= 26·67oz$$

GLOSSARY

ABRASIVES

Materials available as wheels, discs and powders for grinding, polishing and cutting all forms of material. Common abrasives include corundum (emery), sand and silicon carbide. Grinding wheels are made by bonding the abrasive grains with ceramic frits, or organics such as rubber and plastics. Diamonds, both natural and synthetic, are also used for grinding very hard materials and are bonded in metal alloys. Enamellers use pumice stone and ground pumice for polishing metals. Abrasive technology is now very sophisticated and includes the use of complex equipment.

ALGINATES

Organic materials used to give strength to clay bodies, glazes and sometimes enamels, and to keep solids in suspension. They are derived from seaweed and are sold as powders or jellies. In glazes and enamel slips alginates are used as the sodium and ammonium salts.

ANATASE

A form of the mineral titania, TiO_2. Other forms are brookite and rutile. Anatase changes to rutile above 700°C and is responsible for certain colouring effects in glazes.

ANHYDROUS

Anhydrous compounds are those free of water of crystallisation. Hydrated salts, for example washing soda, lose their water of crystallisation upon heating and eventually become anhydrous.

ANION

The negatively charged atom or part of a molecule, for example, Cl, NO₃, SO₄. Derives its name from the fact that anions are released at the anode during electrolysis. The positively charged ion or atom is called the cation.

ANISOTROPY

The property of having different physical properties in different directions, such as in crystals or in ceramic articles. Shrinkage may be anisotropic in drying clays, for example.

ANNEALING

A term used in the metal and glass industries to describe the removal of stresses by careful heat processing. The enameller often needs to soften cold-worked metals to facilitate further shaping and the heating involved in the annealing process causes recrystallisation. The effect of the various complicated annealing cycles used by metallurgists is to yield a grain size in the metal that is optimum for the proposed shaping process. In practice the enameller simply has to heat his metals to red heat and allow them to cool. The precise technique is learned by practice and experience. Wires used in *cloisonné* enamelling should be annealed in this way to reduce their springiness and make them lie flat on the base.

BALLMILLS

Cylindrical closed containers used to grind materials into powders. They may be made of steel (lined with some abrasion-resistant materials such as chertstone), of porcelain, and of rubber. The cylinder is mounted so that it can rotate. The material to be ground is put in the cylinder with water (or other medium) and the grinding body (flint pebbles or some suitable hard agents such as porcelain pebbles or slugs). When the cylinder rotates, the pebbles and material are carried up the side of the ballmill and fall down to the bottom. In doing so the pebbles crush and rub the charge, thus powdering it. The speed of rotation, the ratios of water, material and pebbles, and the grinding times all have critical effects on the efficiency of ballmills.

Q

Suppliers of ceramic equipment produce a large range of ballmills for all purposes. Simple bench models, suitable for art potters and enamellers, come in sizes of up to 18in diameter. Industrial ball mills are up to 4ft in diameter.

BASSE-TAILLÉ

A metal enamelling technique usually reserved for silver. The pattern is cut into the metal as a shallow relief and the depressions filled in with enamel, slightly moistened, using a pallette knife. The fired, enamelled article, is smooth because the enamel surfaces are flush with the metal surface. The forming of the cavities and depressions is done either by mechanical means (chasing and engraving) or chemically (etching with acids using wax or asphalt, resistant materials to protect the areas not to be etched). Transparent enamels are normally used, and the effect may be to give the surface a sculptured appearance. The technique requires skill and is used for costly enamelled items made of noble metals.

BAT

Also seen as batt, this term usually refers to a slab or tile of refractory material used in building up supporting shelving inside kilns or on tunnel kiln cars; a bat may also be a piece of plastic clay shaped for subsequent forming on a machine.

BENTONITES

Natural clays derived from weathered volcanic ash. The main mineral in them is montmorillonite—a magnesian clay mineral. Two types of bentonite are common in ceramics: calcium and sodium. The first lacks the distinctive swelling property of the latter—the property for which bentonites are well known. Bentonitic clays are used in small amounts as suspending agents and binders.

BLEBS

Blisters and other protruberances on defective ware.

BLUNGERS

These are machines for mixing clay and water into slips.

They consist of wooden or steel hexagonal or circular vats fitted with paddles that can be rotated at different speeds. The aim of blunging ceramic slips is to produce a uniform, thoroughly dispersed material with the minimum of air entrapment. Blungers and agitated tanks and arks are important units in the pottery slip-house. In small workshops, slips of body, glazes and enamels can be stored without mechanical agitation, but hand paddles should then be used periodically to stir the slips and prevent excessive settling and setting. Slips should not be stored in enamelled metal containers since the electrolytic action of the enamel coating causes rapid settling and setting, especially of ground flint, sand, feldspar and other nonplastics.

BUFFING

This is a metal-finishing process used to smooth and finish copper, steel, etc prior to enamelling. Relatively soft materials such as rubber and fabrics are used at high speeds on grinding wheels to buff metals that are to be enamelled. See also abrasives.

CATION

See anion.

CHAMOTTE

A German word now used throughout the world to denote clay that has been fired. The British and American equivalent term is grog, although the latter also means broken and used refractories, crushed and ground for use as fillers in refractory production or in the manufacture of other types of ceramics. Special kilns are used to calcine clay and kaolins into chamottes for many purposes. 'Grog' may have come from the French *gros grain* (coarse grain).

CHAMPLEVÉ

An enamelling technique in which the pattern is cut quite deeply (compared with *basse taillé*) into the metal before being filled with enamel. The applied enamels are prevented from running and mingling by the borders or fins of uncut metal.

The term, in French, means 'elevated field' which describes the effect in enamelling.

CORDIERITE

A mineral containing magnesium aluminosilicate with iron and often manganese impurities in the crystal lattice. Has a high thermal-shock resistance and is therefore used in oven-to-table pottery and ceramics needing to withstand sudden heat changes. Cordierite is found naturally but it is customary to synthesise it in the ceramic body by firing steatite, alumina and clays. Has a very low thermal expansion.

CURTAINING

A glaze and enamel fault consisting of running of the slips when applied to the ware. The flow properties of the slips need adjusting to eliminate the fault. Occurs on metal enamels as dark patches at rims of ware.

DEGREASING

Before being enamelled, metals must be cleaned and degreased. Old castings and sheet that might have become rusty are often cleaned by sandblasting with sand or chilled iron grit or a similar abrasive. Degreasing may be done either by heating, in the annealing process, which burns off any oily matter, or by immersing in organic and alkali solutions. A common industrial method involves soaking the metal in trichloroethylene but this solvent is expensive and the recovery methods used to reclaim it are only economical on an industrial scale. The metal is then treated with an alkaline cleaning solution containing about 30% caustic soda, 30% soda ash, and other agents such as phosphates, water glass and soap. All metals thus treated are then washed in clean water.

On the scale normally used in art enamelling a hot solution (in water) of 25-30% caustic soda, 25-30% sodium phosphate (Na_3PO_4) and 3-10% water glass is suitable for greasy articles made of steel or iron and also of copper and aluminium. The total weight of chemicals should not be more than 100 gm/litre. The metals are left immersed in the solution at 70-90°C for 10-30 min and then washed in cold water. Care should be taken with this caustic solution.

DIPS

Nickel dips are used in metal enamelling to increase the bonding of metal and enamel. The process, which involves electrochemical processing, is only of industrial interest.

DOPES

Chemical agents used to adjust the rheological properties of clay, glaze and enamel slips. Many such agents are known, such as ammonium chloride, vinegar, hydrochloric acid, tannates, and so on. The term is also used to refer to the addition of minerals to bodies especially in the refractories industry, these agents having considerable effects on the formation of new minerals in the body.

DUNTING

Cracking and splitting of pottery bodies caused by cooling the ware too fast after firing. May occur in biscuit or glost. The The cracks may be invisible but dunting is detected by tapping the article and listening for the characteristic 'ring' of sound ware.

EFFLORESCENCE

This is the name given to scum formation on bricks and other building materials after they have been laid in a wall. The rainwater soaking into the brick and drying out, brings the soluble salts in the brick (or mortar), or even in the soil surrounding the brick to the surface, and upon evaporation deposits the scum there. The efflorescence may contain calcium, magnesium, sodium and potassium sulphates. Hydrochloric acid solutions can be used to remove the white scum, although if the brickmaking clays contained a lot of soluble salts it may take years before they are all leached out of the brickwork.

ELECTROLYTES

This is the term used to describe dissolved salts. The properties and classes of electrolytes are very important to the potter and enameller, since very small amounts have critical effects on the behaviour of clays, glazes, enamels etc. For example, see the discussion on Casting Slips in Section 2.

Chemically, an electrolyte is a compound which when dissolved in water produces ions that may carry electric charges, making them susceptible to electrolysis, and electrophoresis, that is, processes involving the movement of ions in solution or colloidal systems during the passage of electric currents.

ELUTRIATION

When particles of matter such as clay or milled quartz are mixed with water and allowed to settle, they do so according to their size and density. Usually the denser particles settle first. This behaviour is used in the purification of kaolins and clays by settling and also in determining the particle-size distribution of milled quartz, feldspar and glazes. One test is known as the Andreason Pipette method; another, the hydrometer method. For instance, if a cylinder is filled with water containing a few grams of milled flint and a small volume of a deflocculent such as 'Calgon', upon standing, the larger particles will settle out, leaving the fine grains in suspension. A hydrometer can then be used to measure the specific gravity of the liquid (a very thin 'slip') remaining in the container. This value can then be used in calculations based on Stokes' Law to determine the percentage of particle sizes below a certain diameter in the milled material. The test is commonly used in the pottery industry for checking ballmill grinding of nonplastics. The result is reported as 'percentage particles less than 0·01mm'.

ENGOBES

These are coatings of clay or prepared body on clayware, usually designed to approve the appearance of a coarse or badly contaminated underbody. Engobing is a technique also used in fine pottery to decorate tableware with differently coloured bodies. The coloured slip is sprayed on to the greenware, followed by drying and firing. Usually the engobe is more densely vitrified than the underbody and its properties are intermediate between glaze and porous body. Engobing was once a common technique in making santitaryware from fireclay, the finer engobes being used to hide the iron-stained fireclays before the glaze was applied.

EUTECTICS

If two compounds such as alumina and silica are mixed and heated, the mass will be found to fuse at a lower temperature than either of these compounds heated alone. A eutectic mixture is that combination of components with the lowest fusing point for any combination of the compounds. The formation of eutectics is therefore very important in glass making, in glaze and enamel forming and in the firing of clays.

EXOTHERMIC

Exothermic reactions are those in which heat is given off as a result of thermochemical changes occurring in the heated materials. Those reactions which take in heat are called endothermic. The detection and measurement of endo- and exothermic reactions in clays and minerals constitutes the technique of differential thermal analysis (qv).

FAIENCE

Derived originally from the name of earthenware made at Faenza, Italy. Today it refers to any porous earthenware with a glaze on it. The original faience was coated with tin glazes.

FETTLING

This is a term used in pottery to indicate the finishing and sponging of the clayware after forming. In metallurgy, fettling is used to mean the repairing of hearths in furnaces by throwing refractory powders into the furnaces while they are still hot. The heat then fuses the material sufficiently to make a new hearth, ready for further metal production.

FLOCS

Coagulated particles, usually in clay or glaze slips. The term 'flocculate' means to cause the particles to coagulate in the suspension; the term deflocculate means to cause the particles to come apart, thus increasing the flowing power of the slip. See Casting Slips and Deflocculation.

GROGS

See chamotte.

HALLOYSITE

A clay mineral of the kaolinite group but with a distinct particle shape of scrolls instead of platelets. This causes the ware made from such clays to collapse suddenly during firing.

HARDENING-ON

When ceramic colours have been applied to biscuit ware (clayware fired once without glaze) using oils and other organic media, it is sometimes necessary to burn out the media before applying the glaze on top of the decoration. This low-temperature (600-700°C) heat treatment is called 'hardening-on'. During the process, the oils burn out and the small amount of fluxes in the colours bond the decoration to the biscuit ware. Many modern colour-organic formulations do not need hardening-on because the media are based on non-carbonising resins and oils that leave the ware during the glost firing without forming carbon, a reaction that normally causes faults in firing such as blistering.

HYDROFLUORIC ACID

A dangerous mineral acid with the formula HF. It is a solution of hydrogen fluoride in water which can be used to etch glass and glazes.

ILLITE

A group name for certain micaceous clay minerals. The name derives from Illinois, USA, where the minerals were first detected. Illitic clays are those with argillaceous sediments classed in the mica group.

INSULATION

Kilns and furnaces used in potting and enamelling are

normally insulated with lightweight porous refractories such as china-clay bricks and asbestos matting, loose-fill powders, etc to prevent too much heat escaping into the atmosphere. The materials are known as insulating refractories. The porous structure of such materials is obtained by adding combustible materials such as sawdust, which are burnt out during the firing of the bricks, or by chemical foaming methods, similar to those used to make foam plastics. Insulating refractories are graded according to the temperatures of service. Hot-face insulating bricks, for example, may be used at temperatures of 1600°C but these are much denser than insulating brick produced for 'backing' purposes at temperatures of about 800°C. There is a carefully investigated relationship between the bulk density, (expressed in gm per cm^3, or lb/ft^3) and the thermal conductivity. The thermal conductivity is a measure of the rate at which the material transmits the heat. Thus, a brick with a high thermal conductivity (denser bricks are more heat conducting than porous bricks) will allow large quantities of heat to escape through the kiln structure. Insulating power in a material is inversely proportional to the thermal conductivity.

IRON EARTHS

These are a class of materials which contain ochres, siennas and umbers. They are variable in composition and especially in impurity content, depending on their geographical location. Yellow ochre, for example, is a clay containing hydrated ferric oxide. Red ochre contains anhydrous ferric oxide, while umber contains hydrated manganese oxide as well as hydrated ferric oxide. Sienna contains less manganese than does umber. These materials are used for staining bodies and, when ground and sieved to remove coarse impurities, produce uniformly stained bodies. Thieviers earth, found in France and elsewhere, for example, contains 10% Fe_2O_3 and gives a pleasing flesh colour in earthenware bodies. The colours obtained with iron earths are usually very stable even when fired at temperatures as high as 1400°C. The advantage of iron earths for use as pottery pigments is that they are normally more stable than artificial pigments (prepared stains) formulated by blending, for example, iron oxide and titanium dioxide.

LAWNS

See screens.

LIGNIN

A term used to describe cellulose-like substances lining woody fibres in plants and trees. Lignin is often present in clays and forms part of the combustibles which also include coal, peat and similar organic compounds that burn out on firing.

MAJOLICA

Also written maiolica, this was originally porous pottery with a tin glaze. Today the term refers to any porous opacified-glazed ware made at low temperatures.

METAMERIC COLOURS

These are colours that appear to be identical under a single type of illumination, but when placed under a different light source do not match. For example, metal enamels opacified with titania in the rutile mineral form and those with the ana-tase titania form are metameric in natural daylight and artificial light.

MOHS SCALE

A scale of scratch hardness for minerals, ceramics and other materials. The scale is a list of minerals as follows:

1.	Talc	6.	Feldspar
2.	Rock Salt	7.	Quartz
3.	Calcite	8.	Topaz
4.	Fluorspar	9.	Corundum
5.	Apatite	10.	Diamond

Thus, a material that scratches apatite but is itself scratched by feldspar has a Mohs hardness of 5-6. Mohs hardness values give some indication of how diffificult a material will be to grind into a powder. However, this indication is not the only factor of importance. The way a material in lump form breaks down and its particle shape is also important in grinding theory.

MONOCLINIC

A term used to describe some crystals and their structure. The monoclinic form has three axes of unequal length, two intersecting obliquely and being perpendicular to the third. Examples are sodium sulphate and oxalic acid.

MONTMORILLONITE

See bentonites.

PATE-SUR-PATE

A pottery technique in which clay slip is painted in mounting layers on to the clay ware to form a raised motif. The expression means 'paste-on-paste' and originated in early productions of hard paste porcelain. Each application of paste (slip) must be allowed to dry to the leather hard state before the second is applied. Some kind of organic bond is often used in the slips to make them adhere to the ware. The article is fired biscuit before glazing and sometimes is not glazed at all.

P.C.E. (PYROMETRIC CONE EQUIVALENT)

This is a term used particularly to describe the main property of refractory materials. It is a measurement of the fusion point. The 'cone' referred to is usually a Seger cone or similar standard composition which when heated under controlled conditions (temperature and atmosphere) fuses and bends over so that its peak touches the base on which it stands. Thus, if a similar cone is shaped from a new clay or other 'unknown' material and fired alongside the standard cones, by comparing the behaviour we can assign a P.C.E. value to the new material.

Ceramic suppliers produce cones to cover fusing points of from about 600°C to 2000°C. The three main series of cones used in Britain, Europe and the USA are Seger cones, Staffordshire cones, and Orton cones. Cones are a form of pyroscope (see below). They measure the amount of heat-work done on the body being heated and time as well as temperature is critical. Furnace atmospheres need also to be controlled if consistent results are to be obtained.

pH VALUES

This is a symbol indicating the degree of acidity or alkalinity of a solution. Thus on a scale of 1-14, the term $pH = 7$ would denote the neutral point (neither acid nor alkaline). Any values below $pH = 7$ are acid and above, alkaline. The precise meaning of pH is 'the concentration of hydrogen ions in the solution as represented by the logarithm of the reciprocal of the concentration of the hydrogen ions.' All acids contain hydrogen.

pH values are important in the behaviour of glaze and enamel slips and in casting clay slips. Simple kits can be obtained for testing pH values of solutions.

PITCHERS

Broken fired pottery which is often used as a 'filler' or modifying agent in colours, bodies and matting mixtures. The fired pottery is crushed and milled and used in the same way as other nonplastics such as feldspar and flint. However, pitchers cannot be used as substitutes for flint since chemically they are quite distinct.

PLIQUE A JOUR

An enamelling technique in which enamels are applied in the cells formed by metal strips or 'plaits'. The fired article resembles a stained-glass window effect if clear or translucent enamels are used.

PRINTING

Printing techniques are widely used in ceramic decoration, from simple rubber stamping to complex roller and gelatine pad methods. The 'ink' consists of a ceramic stain and an organic vehicle.

PUG MILLS (VACUUM)

These are machines used to remove trapped air from plastic clay. The craft potter kneads and wedges his clay by hand to the same purpose, but for large masses of clay, a small vacuum pugmill is more efficient and obviously less tiring. The pugmill consists of a cylindrical steel barrel containing knives set on a central shaft so that the clay is forced from the feed end to the discharge end when the knives rotate. The clay leaves the pug in a firm, consolidated mass, and (if the job of de-airing is efficient) with greater plasticity than the starting material. Pugmills can also be used without vacuum (de-airing devices but, although these consolidate the clay, they do not remove the air and are thus less useful, since trapped air in plastic clay is the cause of many faults.

PYRITES

This is a generic name for sulphide minerals but in ceramics is normally used to refer to iron pyrites, FeS_2 (iron sulphide). In its most characteristic form iron pyrites is known as 'fool's gold' because of its resemblance to the metal. Other pyrites are 1. copper-pyrite, 2. tin-pyrite, 3. arsenical-pyrite and 4. cobalt-pyrite (smaltite). Pyritic contaminated clays must be treated with care because the soluble salts produced when they are fired (sulphates) may cause a variety of faults such as scumming and adverse deflocculation behaviour in casting slips.

PYROSCOPES

These are devices which when heated in a kiln or furnace alter their appearance in such a way as to indicate the amount of heat-work (time and temperature) done on them. For instance, Seger or Staffordshire cones *(see above)* fuse and bend over when a certain heat treatment has been applied. Buller's rings shink and can be measured after removal from the kiln. Holdcroft bars fuse and bend. Thus, pyroscopes can be placed inside a kiln or furnace and used as a graphic indication of the firing treatment of the ware. By inspecting the state of pyroscopes through spy-holes in the kiln during the cycle, it is possible to decide when the ware is fired. Pyroscopes are normally used in combination with temperature measurements *(see* thermocouples) to give a fairly complete record of the firing cycle.

QUEBRACHO

An extract from the bark of the South American tree of that name. Used as sodium extract for making casting slips that need additional colloidal matter to make them stable. *See also* Tannates.

RAKU

Raku ware is a coarse type of pottery made of a quick-firing porous body and covered with a soft glaze, usually containing lead. The traditional Japanese tea ceremony has made use of raku pots which can be fabricated and fired by the participants immediately prior to using them to drink tea. The open textured body is shaped by hand, dipped in glaze and placed with tongs into a heated kiln, and once-fired at about 750°C. Such ware is obviously mechanically weak and usually crazes within a few hours of leaving the kiln.

RARE EARTHS

These are oxides of rare-earth elements contained in group III of the Periodic System. Oxides of interest to potters and enamellers are used mainly for colours and pigments. They are cerium, yttrium and praseodymium. They are used in glass and enamel making as colourants and for special purposes such as deoxidising the glass.

RATIONAL ANALYSIS

Also known as proximate analysis, this is an arithmetical device used to obtain an indication of the minerals present in clays and other ceramic raw materials from their chemical analysis. The method was until recently based on the assumption that clays contain kaolinite, feldspar and quartz as the main minerals. Thus, by using the potash (K_2O) concentration to calculate the amount of feldspar present, it was possible, in theory, to work out the full mineralogical analysis in terms of these three minerals.

However, it is now known that alkalis such as potassia are present in many clays in the form of mica and not feldspar. So the proximate analysis must now be based on the assumption that the three important minerals are kaolinite, mica and quartz. Modern mineralogical study techniques and the electron microscope have rendered the 'rational analysis' method obsolete, although some ceramists still claim that it can provide useful practical information.

REFRACTORINESS UNDER LOAD

This is the measure of the ability of a material to withstand high temperature heating under a mechanical load. Firebrick and other refractories used in kiln building need to withstand the weight of the bricks laid on top of them in walls, etc, and thus their resistance to heat does not alone indicate how they will behave in service. A special test is used to determine the property, involving the application of steady or increasing loads to a block of the material, and raising the temperature until the block shears or collapses owing to fusion or other forms of failure.

RHEOLOGY

The science of the flow and deformation of materials. Terms such as viscosity, fluidity, thixotropy, shear stress, and so on are used by the rheologist to describe the behaviour of slips, glazes and enamels.

ROPY

Casting slips that congeal on standing and do not flow smoothly in casting are called ropy.

RUTILE

See anatase

SADDLE

A small ceramic support used in kiln furniture for holding ware being glost fired. Usually takes the form of a small bar with triangular section.

SAGGAR

A refractory box or container used for holding ware during firing. Commonly made from fireclay and grog or chamotte. Not now used as often as in the past.

SGRAFFITO

This is a pottery decorating method involving the application of a coloured engobe *(see above)* to the green ware followed by the scratching of a pattern in the engobe layer so as to reveal the underbody, which is normally of a different colour to the engobe. A very popular art potting form.

SIEVES AND SCREENS

These are important parts of potting and enamelling equipment. The main feature of a sieve is, of course, the size of its holes (mesh). Screens are made of different alloys and also of fabric such as nylon and perlon. Sieve numbers indicating the size of the holes in the mesh vary with different countries. In Britain and the USA mesh numbers are different for some sizes but the same for others. Thus the following table shows the figures for some common potter's sieves.

Mesh Aperture, mm	Mesh Numbers		Precise aperture size in USA
	UK	USA	
1·68	10	12	1·68
0·71	22	25	0·707
0·50	30	35	0·50
0·25	60	60	0·25
0·18	85	80	0·177
0·15	100	100	0·149
0·125	120	120	0·125
0·105	150	140	0·100
0·075	200	200	0·074
0·063	240	230	0·063

Example: A material ground in the USA to pass through mesh No 35 would have a maximum particle size of 0·50mm, as in Britain, but the screen number to use in Britain would be No 30.

SILICON CARBIDE, SiC

A highly refractory material used for dense kiln furniture and in many types of furnace lining because of its high thermal-shock (spalling) resistance and its high refractoriness under load (see above). Specks of silicon carbide in pottery bodies and glazes may cause blistering faults and contamination similar to iron specking. New slabs of silicon carbide used as kiln furniture should be washed with kaolin slip before being loaded with glost ware.

SILK SCREENING

A ceramic decorating method involving the application of the ceramic ink through a silk screen, suitably blocked out with organic materials, to form the design. Hand or mechanical forms are commonly used.

SINTERING

This is a complex reaction that occurs between particles of solids without or in the presence of a liquid (flux) phase. The sintering process is said to begin when powders are heated to a temperature below that needed to vitrify the mass but high enough to initiate solid reactions or crystallisation. The obvious result of sintering is an increase in the strength of the powders due to their compaction and densification. The reaction seems to take place, initially at least, at the surface of the particles.

SOLID SOLUTIONS

Just as solids such as common salt and sugar dissolve in liquids like water, it is possible for solids to dissolve in other solids (at high temperatures). The precise definition of solid solutions involves specialised chemical terminology and needs an understanding of the behaviour of crystallization. Thus, a solid solution has been defined as a crystalline phase whose composition can vary without forming a new extra phase.

SPALLING

A term used to describe damage done to ware during sudden heating. May appear as cracking or chipping and flaking of edges and corners. *See also* Thermal Shock Resistance.

SPINELS

These are crystalline compounds, often of great complexity within a common group of minerals possessing the same or similar structures and chemical formulae. The term 'spinel' is also given to one specific compound with the formula MgO. Al_2O_3, which is important as a refractory material, and also because it can be used as a simple pattern for other spinels.

R

Spinels form one of the main classes of colours in ceramics (using the structural concept of classification).

SQUATTING

The collapse through softening under heat of ceramic materials or metals. Usually associated with the behaviour of Seger cones (qv).

TANNATE

Extracts of tannin from the bark of trees. Sodium and other tannates are sometimes used in casting-slip deflocculation and to stabilise clay suspensions. *See* Quebracho.

TEMPERATURE SCALES

The common scales used in science and technology and also in ceramics are 1. Fahrenheit °F; 2. Celsius (often confused with Centigrade) °C; 3. Absolute, °K.

'Degrees Absolute' is the scale formed simply by adding 273° to the Celsius value.

The Celsius scale readings can be converted to Fahrenheit by using the simple formula

$$\frac{C° \times 9}{5} + 32 = \text{Degrees Fahrenheit}$$

Example: To change 560°C to degrees Fahrenheit, that is

$$\frac{560 \times 9}{5} + 32 = 1040°F$$

Fahrenheit temperature readings can be changed to Celsius by using formula

$$\frac{F - 32}{9} \times 5 = \text{Degrees Celsius (°C)}$$

Example: Change 820°F to °C

$$\frac{820 - 32}{9} \times 5 = 438°F$$

THERMAL SHOCK RESISTANCE

Also known as spalling and dunting resistance. It is a measure of a material's ability to withstand sudden heating or cooling. When a pot, for instance, is broken by rapid cooling or heating, the damage is due to its inability to stand the stresses set up in it by the thermal gradients (temperature differences in different parts of the article). The thermal-shock resistance of pottery also plays a role in the crazing test used in many potteries. For example, ware is often craze tested by immersing steaming hot ware in cold water. The resulting crazing of the glaze, if any, is due to a combination of thermal shock and the expansion of the ware, due to the absorbing of moisture into its pores. The glaze, normally under compression on the body, cannot stand the tensile forces of the expanding body and gives way, thus causing the glaze to craze, that is, to crack.

WREATHING

A fault in casting slips usually taking the form of a series of corrugations inside the cast hollow ware. The rheology of the slip needs to be adjusted to eliminate this fault.

BIBLIOGRAPHY

Practical Instruction

Billington, Dora. *The Technique of Pottery* (1962)
Cardew, Michael. *Pioneer Pottery,* (1969)
Clark, Kenneth. *Practical Pottery and Ceramics* (1964)
Drawbell, Marjorie. *Making Pottery Figures* (1961)
Fieldhouse, Murray. *Pottery* (1956). New edition in preparation
Leach, Bernard. *A Potter's Book* (1945)
Marlow, Reginald. *Pottery Making and Decoration,* London and New York (1957)
Various Authors. *The Manual of Practical Pottery,* Smith and Greenwood (1893-4)
Winter, Edward. *Enamel Arts on Metals,* Cleveland, Ohio, (1958)
Winter, Edward. *Enamel Painting Techniques,* London and New York (1971)
Winter, Thelma F. *Ceramic Sculpture* (1971)

Scientific and Theoretical Works

Andrews, A. I. *Porcelain Enamels,* Illinois (1961)
Budnikov, P. P. *The Technology of Ceramics and Refractories* (1964)
Dale, A. J. *Modern Ceramic Practice* (1964)
Dodd, A. E. *Dictionary of Ceramics* (1964)
Ford, R. W. *Drying* (1961). Institute of Ceramics textbook series
Ford, W. F. *Effect of Heat on Ceramics* (1967). Institute of Ceramics textbook series
Fraser, H. *Kilns and Kiln Firing for the Craft Potter* (1969)

Griffiths, R. and Radford, C. *Calculations in Ceramics* (1965)

Kingery, W. D. and Wiley, J. (Editors). *Ceramic Fabrication Processes* (1958)

Moore, F. *Rheology of Ceramic Systems* (1965). Institute of Ceramics textbook series

Rado, Paul. *An Introduction to the Technology of Pottery* (1969)

Shaw, Kenneth. *Ceramic Colours and Pottery Decoration* (1968, 2nd Ed)

Shaw, Kenneth. *Ceramic Glazes* (1971)

Vargin, V. V. *Technology of Enamels* (1967)

Worrall, W. E. *Raw Materials* (1965). Institute of Ceramics textbook series

Journals and Associations

Ceramic Age, 2800 Euclid Avenue, Cleveland, Ohio 44115, USA

Ceramic Industry, South Wabash Avenue, Chicago, Illinois 60603, USA

Ceramic Review, Magazine of the Craftsmen Potters' Association of Great Britain, 5 Belsize Lane, London NW3 5AD

Ceramics, Arrow Press Ltd, 65-66 Turnmill Street, London EC1

Journal of the American Ceramic Society, (also the *Bulletin* for practical matters) 4055 N. High Street, Columbus, Ohio 43214, USA

Tableware International, John Adam Street, Adelphi, London WC2

Transactions of the British Ceramics Society, Shelton House, Stoke Road, Shelton, Stoke-on-Trent

Organisations

British Ceramic Research Association, Penkhull, Stoke-on-Trent

Institute of Ceramics, Shelton House, Stoke Road, Stoke-on-Trent

INDEX

INDEX   261

Vinegar in clays, 86
Viscosity, 55, 98
Vitrification, 53, 186, 188
Vitrification range, 42, 54
Vitrifiable clays, 15
Volatilisation, 47

Warping of clay, 176
Water as raw material, 72
Water absorption, 230
Water glass, 100
Wax, 77
Weathering, 28
Wedging clay, 90
Wedgwood, 66, 68, 84, 149, 168
Welding metals, 78
Wet atmospheres, 200
Wetting of colours, 23

White hard state, 176
Whiting, 48, 220
Window glass, 114
Winter, Edward, 65
Witherite, 41
Wires, 79
Wires, annealing, 233
Wood as fuel, 201
Wood ashes, 59
Wollastonite, 53, 137, 183
Wreathing, 106. 251

Zinc, 36, 135
Zinc oxide, 125, 128
Zinc sulphate, 154
Zircon, 129, 133
Zircon bat wash, 211
Zirconia, 129

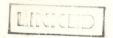